William M. Mathers

History of the Sandusky Conference

William M. Mathers

History of the Sandusky Conference

ISBN/EAN: 9783337036423

Printed in Europe, USA, Canada, Australia, Japan

Cover: Foto ©ninafisch / pixelio.de

More available books at **www.hansebooks.com**

HISTORY

—— OF THE ——

Sandusky Conference

——BY——

WM. M. MATHERS.

TOLEDO, O.:
TOLEDO COMMERCIAL BOOK AND JOB PRINTING,
No. 338 Summit Street.

INTRODUCTION.

The idea of writing a brief history of the Sandusky Conference did not originate with the author. A number of brethren have long felt that such a work was a positive necessity to enable the church of the present to review the ground over which the Conference has passed since its first organization, as the connecting links of the past with the present, are fast dropping out. Brethren at different times were appointed to perform this task, and if they would have undertaken the work we might have had something much better and more worthy of being preserved, and the author of this little book saved the time and labor of its preparation.

At a Ministerial Association, held on the Findlay District, I was appointed by the Association to write some reminiscences of Sandusky Conference. Not being present, I misapprehended their intentions and wrote what I supposed to be the thought of the Association, and read the paper at an Association held at Bethlehem, in the spring of 1887. The production met the approval of the Association, as to quality, but not as to quantity. I was requested to re-write and enlarge with the view of putting it in some permanent form to be preserved by those upon whom the burdens of the church must rest when the Fathers shall have passed to their reward. This I was unwilling to do, not that I believed such a work would not be interesting and useful, but because I felt myself incompetant to write anything that would command the respect of the present enlightened age. At an Association of the Sandusky District held at Chicago Junction, the request was renewed. It was thought that a connection with the Church and Conference for forty-six years, gave me opportunities for writing that few possessed. After mature deliberation, I yielded to the wishes of brethern whose judgment I thought worthy of respect, and now give to the church what I trust will prove to them instructive, and result in glorifying God. It is not claimed that all by whose instrumentality, ministerial abilities and usefullness, the conference has been brought up to its present state of prosperity and usefulness have been noticed; to have done this would have increased it beyond its intended size without increasing its real value.

Having been prompted by no other motives, as I verily believe, than the glory of God, I ask every reader to overlook its many imperfections, and read with that christian charity which characterizes the life of every genuine christian.

W. M.

History of Sandusky Conference.

The United Brethren Church is not a branch broken off from some other church organization as claimed by some, but was the result of a genuine revival of religion, in which Rev. Wm. Otterbein was the prominent leader. He was sent as a missionary to America from Dillenburg, Germany, by the German Reformed Church. His relations with the church of his early choice became very unpleasant because of the formal state of said church and the strong opposition which his plain gospel preaching elicited. Mr. Otterbein had obtained through faith in the Son of God, a clear evidence of the forgiveness of his sins, and from the period of his conversion to the year 1774, and onward, opposition to the revival and to its agents, was bitter and unintermitting, which led ultimately to a final separation from the church. We find him in May, 1774, in the city of Baltimore organizing a separate church to be known as the *Evangelical* Reformed. At this time the name, which the church afterwards adopted, was not thought of, nor that this child of Providence should become a strong man to run a race, carrying the gospel to hundreds of thousands, leading them to a nobler and happier life.

The circumstances which gave rise to the name which the church afterwards adopted, may not be uninteresting. A great meeting had been appointed at Isaac Long's barn in Lancaster County, Pa., to which christians of all denominations were invited. At this meeting Otterbein and Boehem met for the first time. They were both in the vigor of manhood. Boehem was of small stature, wore his beard long and was dressed in the plain Mennonite costume. Otterbein, on the contrary, was a large man of commanding person, wearing the ordinary clerical dress. There was a striking contrast in the *personal* of the two men. Boehem preached the first sermon; at the close of which, and before he had time to resume his seat, Otterbein arose and folding him in his arms said,

"WE ARE BRETHREN."

The effect produced can better be imagined than described. Many praised God aloud, while the greater part were bathed in tears, and all hearts seemed melted into one. The result of this meeting under the influence of the Holy Spirit, was to unite christians of different orders more closely together in one common brotherhood, giving rise for the fourth time, to the name, "UNITED BRETHREN."

Early in the fifteenth century a church was formed in Bohemia, Germany, similar to that of the Waldenses, calling themselves United Brethren. In the sixteenth century a part of the German Reformed church united with the Waldenses, and formed what was called the Church of the United Brethren. Still later was organized the Church of the Moravians or the renewed United Brethren. These churches, though calling themselves by the same name, had no ecclesiastical connection. On the 25th of September, 1800, the conference assembled at Peter Kemp's in Frederick County, Md. Up to this period the church had passed under the name of UNITED BRETHREN, but it was suggested at this conference, in view of the fact that there was other churches bearing the same name, to avoid difficulties in executing wills, deeds, and other legal instruments, the additional phrase, "IN CHRIST" was added. Hence since 1800 the proper name of the denomination has been.

THE CHURCH OF THE UNITED BRETHREN IN CHRIST.

In order to systematize and give greater efficiency to the work upon which God had set his seal, annual conferences were organized, at which the preachers in said districts met to consult and lay plans for future work in the Lord's vineyard

In 1825 there was four annual conferences, to-wit: Pennsylvania, Miami, Muskingdom and Scioto, organized in the order here given. Scioto being set off by the General Conference of the same year. In 1833, Sandusky was added to the list, making seven in all. The conference has made a record of which it need not be ashamed; one that will serve as an incentive to greater activity in rescuing the perishing, and in building up the church of Christ.

The first member of the United Brethren Church that lived in the territory embraced in the bounds of this conference, so far as we have any knowledge, was Rev. Jacob Baulus, one of the earliest and most efficient preachers in Maryland. He settled near Lower Sandusky (now Fremont) in 1822. His home was located in the deep dark forest of the Black Swamp. In opening up a farm he was not unmindful of the spiritual wants of the people, but commenced preaching to the new settlers as the opportunity offered itself. He also opened his house, and spread his table for ministers of other denominations. A few preaching places were established; a few classes organized, and in 1829 the General Conference located a circuit in that section, and called it Sandusky Circuit. At the next session of the Muskingdom Conference, Jacob Baulus was elected presiding elder of the Sandusky District, and J. Zahn was appointed to take charge of the circuit. The following year Mr. Baulus was re-elected presiding elder, and Israel Harrington and J. Harrison assigned to the Sandusky circuit. These four, Zahn, Baulus, Harrington and Harrison, are said to have been the first pioneer itinerant preachers of this church in Northwestern Ohio. Between this time and 1833, a number of United Brethren families moved into this territory, and among them some excellent local preachers. George Hiskey settled near Lexington, Richland Co.; Henry Errett and John Smith near Galion, Crawford Co.; Phillip Cramer west of Findlay, Hancock Co.; Israel Harrington who was placed on the circuit in 1830, located on the Portage river; while Henry Kimberlin and John and Jacob Crum settled on Bever Creek, Wood Co. These were all good men, and were not only instrumental in leading many to Christ, but have left influences that will be felt to the end of time. The grand work done by these pioneers, prepared the way for a conference, so the General Conference which met at Dresbach's Church, Pickaway County, Ohio, May 14th, 1833, set off the Sandusky work as a separate conference. The new conference held its first session at the house of Phillip Bretz, on Honey Creek, Seneca Co., May 12th, 1834. Bishop Heistand organized the conference, and the following ministers were present: Jacob Baulus, George Hiskey, Jeremiah Brown, C. Zook, John Crum, W. T. Tracy, Jacob Bair, O. Strong, Henry Errett, J. Smith, Lawrence Easterly, Phillip Cramer, J. Alsop, Benjamin Moore, Daniel Strayer, Israel Harrington, Jacob Crum, Henry Kimberlin and John Fry; twenty in number, all of whom have passed to their final reward. At this early day no statistics were kept of members received, so that we have no means of knowing what the membership was, or how rapidly it increased.

The following brethren were admitted at its first session: John Davis, Jacob Garber, Stephen Lilebridge, A. Winch, J. C. Rice and B. F. Kauffman. Mr. Lilebridge did more perhaps than any other man of his day to build up the cause of Christ in the Sandusky conference. He was born January 31st, 1815, and in his 18th year experienced the pardon of his sins and united with the church. In a very short time he was moved to call sinners to repentance, and for eight years he served the church faithfully as an itinerant. Few can realize at this time, the privations and hardships of a pioneer missionary in this sparsely settled country, without bridges and but few roads, sometimes on horseback, and not unfrequently afoot. "To go where the brethren as yet had no name nor home, and where Christ was seldom preached by any minister, and still less known, was his peculiar call, as it was his pleasure and delight." During the eight years of his itinerancy, his annual pay was less than one hundred dollars, with but one single exception. He suffered much from the want of suitable clothing during the winter season, which was one of the causes of his untimely death From his diary it appears that during his brief carear he preached 1930 sermons. After forming many new societies, and winning hundreds to Christ, at the early age of 28, on the 25th of May

1843 he died, near Findlay, O., and was buried in the old grave yard on the east side of town. When the writer was stationed in Findlay, just sixteen years later, he found the grave in a dilapidated condition, with nothing but a board to mark his grave; going out into the country, preaching and taking up collections in different congregations money enough was secured to place at his grave a suitable tombstone; subsequently his remains were removed to the new cemetary west of town, where they now rest, waiting the summons of the master from on high.

Jacob Garber, another of the members received at this first conference has always been the fast friend of the church; being a man of unblemished character he now shares largely the confidence of his brethren. Part of this time he served as an itinerant and part of the time in a local relation, but whether local or traveling, he was always ready to assist in building up the cause of the Redeemer. He is now 94 years of age, lives in Charlotte, Mich., is able to preach occasionally, and to attend the house of the Lord, in which he takes great delight. The second conference was held at the house of Adam Beck's in Crawford Co., April 15th, 1835, Bro. Heistand was the presiding bishop. At this time there was not a church house in the bounds of the conference, and for some years they were held in private houses, and school houses. The first churches owned by the conference was in Lexington, Richland Co., the stone church on Honey Creek, and Bethel near where Burgoon now stands, but which one was first in point of time, I have not the means at hand at present to determine. The following brethren were licensed to preach the gospel: Jacob Newman, J. Logan, J. Bever and J. Dorcas. H. G. Spaythe was received on transfer. James Nighman and Henry Purdy came into the conference about this time, but the minutes gives no account of it. Brother Newman began the work of the ministry in 1833, and for twenty years labored in the Sandusky conference. In 1853 he emigrated to Iowa where he continued in the itinerant work until the weight of years compelled him to retire from the active field. He was a preacher in the church 47 years, 37 of which was spent in active service as an itinerant. He died at the age of 80 in the full assurance of immortality and eternal life.

Brother Bever spent many years in the regular work, sometimes on circuits, and sometimes as Presiding Elder, but in whatever relation, his labors were highly appreciated by the people. He is now upon the shady side of life, surrounded with all the comforts of a pleasant home, and in the full confidence of the church, waiting the Masters own time.

The following year the conference was held at the house of brother Crum, in Wood county, commencing April 26, 1836. Bishop S. Heistand presiding.

Michael Long, C. Tug, D. Strayer, A. Spracklin and *John Long were licensed to preach. Bro. Spracklin became a very able preacher, and for many years was a faithful intinerant. The few last years of his life were spent in a local relation, on a farm near Kenton, *where life's last battles were fought*, her victories won, and he entered into rest. Bro M. Long has traveled longer and suffered more privations in the conference than any other man, living or dead, and has succeeded in bringing thousands into the church; for fifty-one years he has taken work from the conference, with the exception of one or two years; he has never missed a single session. At the session held in Bascom, in 1886, feeling the years bearing somewhat heavily upon him, took a local relation, but since that time has rendered valuable assistance to some of the brethren, and his burning zeal for the Master's cause will enable him to gather many sheaves for the garner above. The following year the conference was held at Lexington, Richland county. Bishop Heistand opened the conference April 11th, 1837, and the following brethren were received. P. Newman, Josiah Linsey, J. Feller and F. Clymer. The conference for 1838 was held at Union school house, Seneca county, commencing April 25th. J. Erb was the Presiding Bishop. Union school house was three miles north of Tiffin, in the

---

*There is a difference of opinion as to whether he joined at this conference, or the year before; the minutes are silent.

Stoner neighborhood, where at one time we had a flourishing society, but by deaths and removals the society has become extinct, and the ground is occupied by others. Jonathan Thomas and J. Spracklin were licensed to preach.

Up to this time the amount of salaries had not been given. The following may be somewhat interesting to those who are so much concerned about their salaries: B. F. Kaufmann, $41.58; J. Davis, $160.00; J. Alsop, $93.00; J. Dorcas, $77.80; J. Thomas, six months, $28.00; S. Lilebridge, $89.00; J. Lindsey, $15.00; B. Moore, $40.87. The next conference was held at the same place, and there was not a single applicant for license to preach, a thing unprecedented in the history of the conference; J. Erb was the Bishop. The next session was held at the house of Phillip Bretz, Seneca Co., March 11th, 1840, and was opened by J. Erb, Bishop. Wm. Furgason and B. J. Needles were the only members received at this conference. It may seem a little strange now, that slavery has been dead nearly a quarter of a century, that an anti slavery church should pass such a resolution as the following: Resolved, "That the Religious Telescope be silent upon the subject of slavery." This was not however because they believed slavery to be right, but because of the persecution through which the church had to pass in Virginia, because of its anti-slavery sentiments which the Telescope proclaimed; not wishing to stir up bitter feeling against the church unnecessarily, was the cause of the passage of this resolution. But in 1848, just eight years later, they were convinced that silence in the presence of a potent enemy was sin, so they passed the following resolution: Resolved, "That we believe it to be anti-christian and contrary to good gospel principle for any one to oppose our preachers and others in preaching and lecturing against the great moral evils of the day, such as slavery, war, intemperance, and secret societies."

The conference held it next session at King's School House, Richland Co., April 27th, 1841; Jacob Erb, presiding Bishop. The following brethren were admitted to membership. J. C. Bright, Alonzo Butler, Wm. Atkinson, Peter Flack, Wm. L. Smith, and Wm. McDowel. The name of Alonzo Butler takes me back in memory forty-six years, when in the old Lexington Church, I gave him my hand to be received into this church. He has long since entered into rest. At this time there was strong opposition to education, and especially to an educated ministry; so they instructed their delegates to the next general conference to use their influence against innovations of this kind. Resolved, "That we instruct our delegates to the next general conference to use their influence to prevent any measure from appearing in the discipline which would require from the candidates for the ministry a course of preparitory study of classical reading and the the study of natural philosophy as a necessary qualification for the admission into the ministry of our Church."

The amount of salary this year was as follows: J. Thomas, $152.00; S. Lilebridge, $119.00; J. Newman, 127.96; M. Long, $152.70; A. Spracklin, $110.70; Presiding Elder, $28.95; Bishop, $15.00.

The conference at this time was a little tenacious not to say superstitious in regard to the manner in which a minister ought to be attired; whiskers were considered a mark of the beast, and long hair would in no case be tolerated. Many a young minister was shorn of his locks, if not of his strength, to satisfy the wishes of their older brethren. No preacher was properly attired in their estimation, unless he wore a white hat This afforded, "John Davis, the hatter" quite a market for his hats. Bishop Edwards was considerably annoyed, while walking the streets in Boston by the boys calling after him: "The man with the white hat, who skined the cat." The brethren sympathized with the good Bishop, and furnished him with money to buy a black hat. Most any of us would be willing to suffer a little persecution if it should terminate so happily.

About the year 1835 David Landis one of our most efficient laymen from the Miami Conference moved into Defiance County, and through his earnest solicitations, Henry Kumler, Jr., who had just been elected Bishop, opened up a Mission in Defiance and adjoining counties. He went out under the auspices of the Miami Conference; without missionary funds, however. He spent the summer, fall and winter of 1841-'42 on this mission, and succeeded grandly, in building up the church in the Maumee Valley. He also brought a number of ministers into the United Brethren Church who proved themselves efficient helpers in the cultivation of this new field for the church, and for God. Brother Landis was a zealous worker in the vineyard of his master; strongly attached to the church of his early choice, and beloved by all that knew him He lived to see the church spread all over Northwestern Ohio, with large societies and fine churches, having fought a good fight and finished his course, he entered his long sought rest.

Mr. Kumler went to the Sandusky Conference which met at Monclova, Lucas County, April 11th, 1842, and presented the ministers that had become co-laborers with him. They were received and the Maumee Mission recognized as a part of the Sandusky work. H Kumler was the Presiding Bishop. The following brethren were admitted to membership at this session: Joseph Miller, Ezra Crary, John D. Martin, G. W. Chapman, Charles Gardner, A. Eby, S Gruber and P. J. Thornton.

The next conference was held at Bever Creek School House, Wood County, April 28th, 1843.

Bishop Kumler opened the conference, after which the following brethren were received: Joshua Bare, T. Shortass, A. Bottenburg, J. George, Wm. Bevington, D. P. Hurlbut, S. Lindsey, J. W. Mains, G. C. Smith, J. Garn, S. F. Headly, W. Walcott, P. Schlappie, J. Lawrence, and I. Preston; and J. Powel was received on his transfer from Scioot. Samuel Long's name now appears first on the conference journal. He entered the ministry in the Muskingum conference in 1830. From him I received my first license to preach, and my first appointment as an itinerant. He was reserved in his conversation, unassuming in his manners, and no one could be in his company long without feeling that he was a man o deep piety. As a preacher he was above the average; and I have witnessed whole congregations moved to tears as he presented the thrilling truths of the Gospel. For the last eight years of his life he was an invalid, most of that time unable to converse, or feed himself, but was never heard to murmur or complain, but waited patiently the Lord's own time. He died at his home near Kansas, Seneca County, Ohio, September 2d, 1887 at the good age of 85 years, 11 months and 10 days.

Joseph Garn is one of the oldest members now living, he always sustained a local relation, but done much to build up the church in his own community by assisting the itinerants, and preaching to the new settlers as opportunities were presented. He lives at Helena, Sandusky County, and possesses all the zeal of former years, and is only prevented from active work, by the infirmatives of age. His prospects are brightening, as one mile stone after another is passed, urged on by the Saviors own promise, "Be thou faithful until death, and I will give the a crown of life."

At this time camp-meetings were held in different parts of the conference, the want of church houses made this a necessity. These gatherings were looked forward to with a great deal of interest, because they were seasons of refreshing and revival. In the fall of '42 one was held on the land of V. Hiskey, near Lexington, at which about seventy were converted, mostly young people, some of which became very efficient workers in the church. During the alter services one evening, when the alter was packed, an evil disposed man with murderous intent, threw a large stone upon the roof of the preachers stand and then made his escape in the darkness of the night; it came within about two feet of coming over into the alter, where it could scarcely have failed to have killed some one. Rev. G. Hiskey requested from the stand, that christians unite in prayer for the unknown man for six months, that God might bring the perpetrator of such a terrible crime to light. The sequel will show as to whether God answered that prayer or not. Two men were digging a well at Johnsville; one said at the dinner table that he had throwed that stone but they had never found it out. That afternoon the well caved in, and hurried him into eternity, and all before the six months had expired.

The conference of 1844 was held at Rev. Joseph Garns, commencing April 4th, with Bishop Kumler presiding. The following applicants were received: A. Berry, J. Abdell and W. Herrington. At this and the following conference, but little business outside of the regular work of the conference was transacted.

The next session was held at Monclova, Lucas County, April 28th, 1845. No Bishop being present, H. G. Spaythe was elected Bishop pro tem. M. Morthland and W. Hendrixson were licensed to preach, and J. Berger and D. Glancy received on their transfers. The conference began to feel the need of a more thorough preparation for the work of the ministry, so they instructed their delegates to the next general conference to use their influence to have a course of study pointed out for the preachers; and those books best calculated to secure the end in view. Until this time but little stress had been laid upon education. A clear christian experience, soundness in doctrine and a holy life, were the most important and the only things really insisted upon. They are the most important now, but the church has learned that education is an important factor of ministerial character and success.

On the 13th of March, 1846 the conference commenced its next session at the Stone Church on Honey Creek. W. Hanby was the presiding Bishop. Brother Headly having died during the year, the conference felt deeply the loss of so good and faithful a toiler in the vineyard of the Master, and expressed their hearty sympathy with the widow upon whom the affliction fell most heavily. At this time the Presiding Elder's received the eighth dollar of the salary collected on the circuit, and by action of the conference, part of that was to be taken in trade; what kind of trade is not stated, whether potatoes, corn or hay, but I do know that a good sister put a head of cabbage in Brother Newman's "saddle bags" for him to take home to his family, on horseback, only about one hundred miles distant; but that was no more difficult than for Brother Hurlbut to take a quarter of beef on his horse before him, which he did, when it was offered to him by a brother who wanted to be liberal, when he thought the gift could not be accepted. But Brother Hurlbut was equal to the emergency, and told him to put it on before him, which he did, a little to his own disappointment, but to the preachers benefit. The following brethren were received on their transfers: C. Allman, J. Miller and I. Pepper.

The next conference was held at the Bever Creek School House, Wood County, February 8th, 1847. Bishop Russel presiding. The most important business that came before the body was a proposition presented by L. Davis of Scioto conference, to co-operate with said conference in buying the Young Men's Seminary at Blendon, Franklin County, Ohio. After a long and heated discussion, in which the leading members took part, pro and con, it was agreed by a small majority, to co-operate with said conference, in buying what is now known as *Otterbein University;* this being the first institution of learning owned by the church. We have now, twenty .colleges and academies. J. Berger, D. P. Hurlbut and P. Flack, were elected its first trustees. E. Crary, Wm. L. Smith and Lawrence Easterly having died during the year, the conference took action, expressive of their appreciation of these dear brethren, and extended to the surviving friends their tenderest sympathies. The following brethren were licensed to preach: D. Cover, P. Tabler, H. B. Winton and J. Brown ; and J. Struble was received on transfer. P. Tabler became one of our most successful revivalists; he served as agent for Otterbein University a number of years; he then moved to Virginia; during the war he enlisted in the army ; at the close of the war he went to Texas on some government business; he wrote to his wife that he had just completed his business and would be ready in a few day to start for home, after which she never heard from him ; his end will remain a mystery no doubt, until the end of time.

Bishop Glossbrenner held the next conference which convened at the Stone Church, on Honey Creek, Seneca County, February 17, 1847. The following applicants were licensed to preach: L. L. Mackey, S. Lee, Wm. Mathers, and C. D. Casey; J. Kurtz and W. Titus were received on their transfers. Brother Casey was a young man of great promise, and the church looked forward to the time when he should become one of its most able defenders, but how soon our fondest hopes are destroyed; by over exertion during a protracted meeting, he was attacked with hemorrhage of the lungs which soon terminated in death. Mr. Lee fully met the most sanguine expectations of the church, and for a number of years was a faithful and successful itinerant. He was our first missionary sent to Michigan, to whose sacrificing toil much of our success is attributable. He continued to labor until declining health compelled him to seek the retirement of home, until called to join the army on the other shore.

Brother Mackey always sustained a local relation; he was a man of fine acquired abilities, a wise counselor and true friend of the church. He has long since entered into rest.

The time of holding the conference was changed from spring to fall, and the next session was held at Walters' School House, Lucas Co., October 20th, 1848. The following brethren were admitted into the conference: J. Shambaugh, E. Day and C.

Briggs; A. Biddle and J. Gooden received on their transfers from Muskingum. Mr. Briggs served the church many years as a faithful, accepted and successful itinerant. He is now living in Dayton, and as the evening shades gather around, his eye is fixed steadily upon the victor's crown, at the end of his earthly pilgrimage. J. Gooden served a number of years in this conference as an itinerant, and then in ———, especially in the southern part, until transferred from the church militant, to the church triumphant. Rev. A. Biddle, is far advanced in life, being seventy-eight years old. He is one of the oldest connecting links of our church, with the times of the fathers of the early part of the century. After spending the best years of his life in building up the church of his early choice, is now living in Galion, Crawford County, surrounded by all the comforts of a pleasant home, in the confidence of his brethren, with the same interest for the prosperity of the church, which characterized the days of his active service in the ministry. Soon his name will drop from the roll on the conference journal, but it will stand forever recorded on God's eternal ledger on high. This conference was held by Bishop Glossbrenner.

The conference beginning to feel the importance of extending its labors beyond its present limits, established a mission in Michigan, calling it Adrain Mission. The whole membership at this time was

3250. There was a net increase the following year of 940.

The next conference was held at Gilboa, Putnam County. Bro. Glossbrenner also presided at this conference, which was held Oct. 5th, 1849. At this conference five were ordained: Tabler, Lee, Mathers, Casey and Kurtz; three of this number have long since passed to their final reward. The conference feeling the importance of a higher standard of ministerial qualification, appointed a committee to formulate some plan by which the young men might become more thoroughly acquainted with the Holy Scriptures. At this same conference, the delegates to the next general conference were instructed to use their influence for the establishment of missions in Oregon, and beyond the Rocky Mountains; this was the first step towards that mission which has brought such grand results for the church and for God. A. P. Bowman was received on transfer, and Wm. Miller, G. G. Nickey, E. M. Bell and R. Wicks were licensed to preach. Bro. Nickey after traveling four years in Sandusky conference, joined Rock River conference by transfer, August 28, 1856. He was elected Presiding Elder the same year. When Wisconsin conference was formed in 1857, he became a member of the same. This embraced the entire State. He served as Presiding Elder twenty-three years, and in thirty-five years of travel did not miss a single annual conference. Some idea may be formed of the sacrifices which he made to build up the church in that newly settled country, from the following taken from his biography. "In going from one appointment to another he would drive sometimes nearly all day, and see but one or two dwellings. Sometimes when he had gone as far as he could with his team, he would leave it, and go on foot to his quarterly meeting, and often did not get enough in cash at his meeting to pay the bill for the care of his team." "He that goeth forth and weepeth, bearing precious seed, shall doubtless come again with rejoicing, bringing his sheaves with him."

The following conference was held at Honey Creek, Seneca County, presided over by Bishop Edwards, September 20th, 1850. A. Lee, J. K. Judge, S. Kelso, J. N. Martin, T. T. Rose, Wm. Loveless and G. W. Miller were licensed to preach.

The next conference was held by Bishop Edwards the Bever Creek church, Wood County, September 2th, 1851, when the following brethren were received, H. W. Downey, H. Rathburn, J. Loar, B. Straub, D. Wicks, J. Lilley and J. Nixon; E. C. Wright and J. Wright on their transfers. The past year had been one unprecedented in the history of the conference by the loss of members by death. J. M. Crum, C. D. Casey, J. Baulus, T. Shortass and Robert Weeks had been its victims. Two of that number, Casey and Weeks, had just commenced a life of usefulness, and why they should be taken away so soon from the field of toil, in which they gave such promise, must remain a mystery until the mists shall be cleared away by the purer light of heaven. The other three had spent a full day in the vineyard of the Lord, and gathered many sheaves for the garner above.

The conference of 1852 convened in Johnsville, Morrow County, September 16th, with Bishop Edwards in the chair. The following were admitted to membership: A. Miller, T. B. Chase, J. Gear, James Long, P. P. Landon, G. Fox, L. Warner, and J. Murrell; G. Schneider, M. Leonard, J. Fink and J. F. Seiler were received on their transfers. Brother Seiler has shown himself a workman approved of God, and has succeeded in leading many into the fold of Christ. Since he has been unable to take regular work, has rendered valuable assistance to the preachers in their protracted meetings. Soon the last sermon will be preached, the last victory won, and he shall enter into rest.

At this conference a Foreign Missionary Society was formed, with the view of sending the Gospel to the heathen; after some stirring remarks by Bishop Edwards, the amount of $656.00 was secured to carry out this grand and glorious end. A request was also made that the general conference which was to meet the next May, should take definite action upon the subject of Foreign Missions. After mature deliberation, they adopted the plan formulated by the Sandusky conference, with but very little change; so that to this conference belongs the honor of setting in motion agencies that have increased the membership of this church from 40,000 to 195,000 in the short space of thirty-four years, to say nothing of the thousands that have gone from her pale, to join the church triumphant. I cannot refrain from saying that one of the most active agents in bringing about these grand results was Rev. J. C. Bright, of precious memory, who was appointed as the first secretary of the Home Frontier and Foreign Missionary Society of the United Brethren in Christ, who by his solemn appeals stirred the church as it had never been stirred before, until thousands of dollars flowed into its treasury. The conference has always stood in the front ranks of the temperance work, and that the world might understand definitely its position on this question, took the following action: "Knowing the temperance cause to be the cause of God, and believing that in it are found the dearest and highest interest of humanity, and the perpetuation of civil and religious enjoyments; therefore, Resolved, that we as a religious church and people, will use all proper and lawful means to induce our legislators to pass either what is called the Maine law or something equivalent thereto in its features and character, so as to effectually stay immolation of the innumerable sacrifices daily made by the Moloch of intemperance of the interests of the bodies and souls of men." The conference took advanced ground upon the subject of an educated ministry, by requiring of those coming into the ministry the study of Grammar, Whateley's Logic, the Dictionary, also Geography, Natural Philosophy and some approved work on Physiology, but above all they shall be required to read and study the old and new testament.

The next conference was held by Bishop Davis in the Tawa Church, Hancock County, September 14th, 1853. The following brethren were received: R. L. Gray, E. B. Waldo, Wm. L. Kennard, J. H. Knouse, S. Jacoby and W. C. Moffit; M. Bulger and R. Hohn subject to their transfer. At this same conference the Michigan District was taken off, forming a new conference; taking from the parent conference 424 members and 15 preachers. Michigan has now two large conferences, spreading over the entire state.

The next conference was held at Marion, commencing October 4th, 1854, Bishop Edwards presiding. The following candidates for the ministry were presented, and after examination were licensed to preach: J. French, S. Essex, B. W. Day, J. Bell and Wm. Jones. The reports showed a decrease in members of 146. This grew out of the inaccuracy of former reports. The whole membership at this time being 5,399.

The next conference was held with the church at Newville, DeKalb County, Ind., commencing September 12th, 1855, J. J. Glossbrenner, presiding Bishop. This was the home of DAVID LANDES, the pioneer of the United Brethren, in the Maumee Valley, and of SOLOMON DELONG, the father of the DeLong's that have done such efficient work in our church. The Wesleyan Methodist having made a proposition to a union between the two churches, the conference expressed itself friendly to co-operation with said church, and appointed two delegates to attend a meeting the following May to consider the propriety of such union. The following preachers were licensed to preach: L. Moore, J. Gring, D. Miller and W. Martin.

On the 18th of September, 1856, the conference commenced its next session in Flat Rock, Seneca Co., D. Edwards, Bishop. The following brethren after examination, were licensed to preach the Gospel: V. Pond, C. Crossland, H. T. Vangorden, D. Homes and S. Foster.

Otterbein University, had from the first the hearty sympathy of the conference, but the cost of educating in the college was so great that the vast majority of our brethren, and especially our preachers were unable to give their children a collegiate education. This the conference claimed must be remedied by the establishing of a well conducted manual labor department. This plan was finally adopted, but to this there were many objections; some were unwilling to labor, then there was too much expense connected with running this department. It proved a a failure and was soon abandoned.

Father Davis received the relation of conference missionary, which relation he sustained during the remainder of his life.

The next conference was held by Bishop Davis in Vanlue, Hancock County, ———, 1857. The conference had become wonderfully stirred up on the subject of missions, to this and the prayers of the church, that God would send forth more laborers into his vineyard, must be attributed the large increase of members received at this session, fifteen in number, viz: H. Cherry, J. Fields, W. T. Tritch, R. French, G. Hoover, T. Osman, R. Traves, H. Black, H. Vangundy, D S. Caldwell, E. H. Curtes, S. A. Myers, N. Hubbard, M. Shesler and S. T. Lane. Four at least of that number have long since passed to their final reward on high. Bro. R. French is perhaps the only one who is yet in the active work. He is an excellent preacher and is doing a grand work for the church and for God. Mr. Lane after many years of faithful and successful itinerant work is living at Rising Sun, Wood Co., a happy, cheerful old man, waiting the chariot of God to convey him to the eternal city, where no shadows shall fall across his pathway, or the sweat of toil drop from his brow. At this confrence our present constitution was formed for the support of our superannuated and worn out preachers, which has proved so helpful to many. Since this time the treasurer has paid out to those different claimants $15,053.00. A mission was also opened in the New England States; S. Lindsey and L. Moore were appointed to take charge of this new field. After several years of almost fruitless toil, and the expenditure of thousands of dollars, it was abandoned; not because of any want of efficiency upon the part of those sent out from time to time, for it was supplied by young men, and men of age and experience, such as Crouse, Briggs, More, Lindsey, Caldwell, Downey, Cherry, Kemerer and M. Long, but because the people were so congregational in their feelings and plans, that the itinerant system did not meet with much favor from the people; and there were so many other places where money could be expended with so much better results for the church.

About this time strong efforts were being made by politicians to extend the cause of slavery into territories then free, therefore the conference felt it due to itself and to the church, that the world know its true position on this question; this it did by a number of resolutions, one of which is presented here: Resolved, "That we look with regret upon the bold attempt to spread the awful curse and crime of American slavery into territories now free, and into all the free states through the influence of the Dred

Scott decision of the Supreme Court of the United States." The following resolution was also past on the temperance question: Resolved, "That he who sells his grain for the purpose of being distilled into spiritous or malt liquors, except for medicinal or mechanical purposes, is an accomplice in the crime of willful homicide, and if proven should be dealt with accordingly as in any other offense of equal magnitude."

The next conference was held at Liberty Chapel, Henry County, October 7th, 1858, Bishop L. Davis presiding. The following brethren were received: G. Bender, I. Wheeler, Wm Johnson, O. L. Howard, J. Zimmerman, Jas. Mapes, C. O. Lawrence, C. L. Barlow, D. W. Downey, L. J. Osburn, G. Struble, J. Johnson and J. Crum; S. F. Altman and J. Degmeir by transfer from their different conferences. It was found in the course of examination, that a number of the members had joined the Freemason's; among these were some of the leading members of the conference; their number and influence gave them a degree of hope that the conference would be compelled to so modify the rule as to suffer them to retain their membership in the body; but in this they were mistaken. A paper was drawn up offering pardon to all who would confess their wrong, and promise to have no connection with Freemasonary in the future. Some remained obstinate until convinced by the expulsion of one, and the suspension of another, that the conference intended to maintain its law, at whatever sacrifice it might require. All made their confessions and promised to abide by the paper and were heartily forgiven. It is not my purpose to speak here of the moral character of Freemasonary, or any other secret society, but I look upon it as a crime of no small magnitude, for men who take upon themselves the solemn obligations of the ministry and promising in the presence of God and man, to be true to the principles of the church, and execute her laws, to be the first to deliver her into the hands of her enemies; and no one can be guilty in this particular and retain a "conscience void of offence towards God and man."

The next conference was held by Bishop Davis in Carey, Wyandotte Co., commencing October 20th, 1859. Nothing of importance transpired outside the regular business of the conference. The following applicants after being duly examined were licensed to preach the gospel: G. W. Steward, I. Crouse, R. C. Knell, G. French, J. K. Alwood, J. Downing, Wm. Faus, W. T. Watson, N. H. Hale, D. G. Ogden, M. Wilsey, R. Stephens, and J. Crim.

The conference for 1860, was held at Upper Sandusky, Wyandotte Co., September 28th, by Bishop L. Davis. The following preachers were received: T. Cross, S. Colter, W. R. Hardwick, A. Rose, H. K. Berry, W. B. Davis, S. Leonard, J. H. Close, S.

D. Kemerer, and J. E. Hughs; J. Bracket and J. M. Piper from other churches, and A. Pendland by transfer. Of this number, T. Cross in some misterious way shot himself while alone in the woods hunting, but a few months after entering upon his first field of labor. No one was present to bear his dying words to his youthful companion. S. Colter enlisted in the army, during the recent rebellion, and while engaged in battle received a wound from which he soon afterwards died, a sad ending of a life that promised so much for the church; perhaps we would have served the master better to have remained in the work of the ministry, but the case is with the Lord. The conference at this time numbered 117, the highest number ever enrolled.

The next conference was opened by Bishop Markwood on the morning of the 17th of October, 1861, in Flat Rock, Seneca County. The most important feature of this conference was the number of complaints against its members, expulsions, and withdrawals. Among the latter was A. Berry, S. Kelso, H. Vangundy and M. Wilsey. The following brethren were received: D. Zigler and T. D. Ingle; A. A. Shesler was received on transfer. The general conference of 1861, so changed our boundaries as to take from us the entire Maumee District, in which division we lost 24 preachers and 2,463 members.

The conference held its next session at Liberty

Chapel, Crawford Co., October 25th, 1862. Bishop Markwood held the conference assisted by Bishop Edwards. The following from the report on Moral Reform, is worthy of a place here: "Whereas, some of our people are in the habit of spending the christian sabbath in visiting and criminal recreation; Resolved, that we admonish those quietly in these respects to desist therefrom; but in case they persist in such violation of the Holy sabbath, we, as ministers shall feel it to be our duty to execute upon the offending person or persons, the rule of discipline." Rev. Wm. Faus having died during the year, the conference took the following action: "Whereas, It has pleased the Allwise disposer of events, to remove our faithful and beloved brother, Wm. Faus, from labor to reward, during the past year; therefore, Resolved, that while we humbly submit to all the dispensations of His hand, yet we feel deeply our loss, and deplore his early removal from a field of usefulness and efficiency in the great work of saving souls. Resolved, further, that we do mingle our sorrow with his bereaved widow and children, and commend them to the protection of Him who is the widows husband, and a father to the fatherless. Resolved, that in token of our smpathy, an order be drawn on the treasurer of the Benevolent Fund Society, for the sum of $50.00 for the special benefit of sister Faus, and her children. Applicants received: B. Struble, A. M. Steman, S. Klotts, B.

Vanvolkenburg, A. Buckingham and T. Carrol. The thirty-first session of the conference was held at the Honey creek Chapel, Seneca county, October 2, 1863, Bishop Markwood presiding. This was the most stormy one I ever attended, being held at the time when our country was in the throes of death brought about by the slave-holders rebellion. Fiery speeches were made and bad feeling was stirred up until the very life of the church was threatened, but God brought us through the firey ordeal purer and brighter and better. The following resolution the last of a number passed shows pretty clearly the temper of the conference: "We are determined by the grace of God to preach a gospel of liberty among the people, to bear witness to liberty as founded in religion; we will not be put down; we will not be intimidated by political threats; we will not be stopped by mobs; we say to all solemnly, yet kindly that nothing shall turn back this testimony that God made man to be free." Four of the leaders in these discussions, Bright, Glancy, Markwood and Rose, have joined the army on the other shore, but not until they saw the collapse of the Southern confederacy and the flag of freedom weaving over every State in the Union, I think a more conservative policy would have succeeded better in holding the church together, such at least was my experience, others thought differently. The following preachers were licensed: F. N. Clymer, R. Cole,

A. Morehouse and A. H. Leonard. There was a decrease in the membership of 183. This was caused no doubt by the unsettled state of the country, one of the results of the cruel war then raging between the North and South.

Bishop Markwood held the next session of the conference at Clear Fork, Richland Co., commencing Sept. 1, 1864. D. Steward, T. J. McKean, J. W. Rhoads, W. F. Clippenger and J. C. Mudge were licensed to preach. The most important work of this conference was the formation of a constitution and by-laws to give more system and greater efficiency to the work of the Sunday School with a request that the General Conference adopt it, which they did with but little alteration. To this we owe much of our success in bringing the Sabbath School up to what it is in our church today, this was timely for the Sabbath School cause had been sadly neglected, there was not a Sabbath School in the conference when I first came into the church within my knowledge.

On the 31st of August, 1865, the conference convened to hold its thirty-third session, in Fostoria. Bishop Edwards presiding, death had again invaded our ranks, and T. T. Rose, one of our most useful itinerants in the midst of his years, and usefulness, was removed from the field of toil and conflict, to the home prepared for all the faithful servants of God. Twenty-two years ago the use of organs in our church was considered an innovation, and this conference felt itself called upon to raise a warning voice against their use, which it did by the following resolution. ("Resolved that it is the sense of this conference that the use of a Mason and Hamlin organ in the Chapel of Otterbein University during Divine worship, is a violation of the discipline of our church, and we respectfullly ask for its discontinuance.") What wonderful changes the last twenty years have wrought; many of them for the better possibly some for the worse, it would be difficult to tell the number used in our churches now. The following resolution was passed which I believe ought to be the rule of the church. Resolved, that every minister in this conference be required to have his name recorded on the class book of the society nearest to where he lives. J. Bell, J. Fry and J. Mathews were received as applicants and Wm. Nevil on his transfer from Muskingum.

On the 30th of August 1866, the conference met in Shelby, Richland Co. and was opened by Bishop Edwards, by the usual religious services. Rev. J. C. Bright had died a short time before the setting of this conference, he had attended the conference in Fostoria, in usual health and received as his appointment Galion station. He found the work in a low religious state and went to work with his usual zeal to promote a revival and build up the church to which he had given the best years of his life. As a result of these special efforts a gracious revival followed, making it one of his most successful years in the ministry, but he so over-taxed himself that he contracted disease, which finally caused his death, although compelled to give up the work to which he was so much attached, and realizing that he must soon be separated from a devoted wife and loving children, he bore his intense sufferings without a murmer or complaint, waiting patiently the Lords own time. A short time before the last summons came, while suffering intensely he said, "If this be dying, it is sweet to die," then after singing this beautiful stanza, "We'll wait till Jesus comes and we'll be gathered home." He entered the golden gate of the city, where the tear of sorrow ne'er dims the eye, and where life's shadows shall never fall across his pathway. A funeral sermon was preached by Rev. A. Biddle in the church where he served his last congregation after which the remains were taken to the cars and conveyed to Columbus, and buried in Green Lawn Cemetery near the city, to await the resurrection of the just. The following brethren were admitted to membership in the conference, E. A. Hubbard, E. Rex, J. W. Finney and B. F. Parmer.

The next session of the conference was held in Findlay, Hancock, Co. August 29, 1867, D. Edwards presiding Bishop. The following brethren were received. J. W. Douglas, J. C. Bebe, R.

K. Wyant, T. J. Harbaugh, N. Foltz, A. J. Nicholas, and B. J. Wise, J. W. Hill and D. R. Miller from Auglaze, and D. White from the Protestant church. Excellent resolutions were passed on missions, publishing interests, education, moral reform, and ministerial support, but as is too often the case, to end with their passage.

The conference met in Upper Sandusky, Wyandotte Co. August 27, 1868 to hold its thirty-sixth session. The conference was opened by Bishop Edwards, and according to his usual custom the first half hour was spent in song, service and prayer. Quite a heavy drain was made upon the conference by transfers, yet the number received was equally large so that there was no decrease in membership. The following brethren were transfered D. S. Caldwell, A. J. Nichols, J. Dorcas, P. Flack, R. L. Gray and S. Lee. The following were received: Wm. Thayer, J. C. Prentice, S. H. Raudebaugh and J. A. Biddle. On transfer Wm. Waters, G. H. Franklin, and E. H. Curtis, and C. Wise from the Evangelical Association, and Wm. Wonder from the Lutheran church. H. Kimberlin having died. J. Garber, H.G. Spaythe and J. Davis were appointed a committee to give the expression of this conference in a memorial of the life, labors and death of this faithful servant of God, in the Religious Telescope. Brother Kimberlin having settled on Beaver Creek in an early day did much to build up the church in that newly settled country. He was very benevolent, giving not only much of his time, but of his means as well to build up the church of his early choice. His success in building up the church as well as his financial prosperity was largely attributable to the co-operation and help of his faithful companion who was equally willing to toil and sacrifice for her loving Master. They lived long enough to see a prosperous society, with a good church in which to worship, and after a full day, as gleaners in the harvest field, they sleep side by side in the cemetery near the place where for years they worshiped waiting the welcome applaudet of the Master; "well done good and faithful servant enter thou into the joy of the Lord."

The conference of 1869, was held at Ottawa, Putnam Co, August 30th. The opening services was conducted by Bishop Glossbrenner, consisting of singing, prayer, reading the scriptures and appropriate remarks. The following brethren were licensed to preach the gospel, J. L. Kitchen, A. Powel, W. A. Keesy, W. P. Dicken, P. Berry, J. T. Kiggens, and C. Hepler; and A. W. Holden was received on transfer from Auglaze. These annual gatherings were not always harmonious, being composed of men whose minds in many respects were different from each other and not always actuated by the purest motives, it could not be otherwise. Dissentions were especially numerous at this time as those who were present well remember. There were some serious difficulties to be adjusted, the settling of which called out some hard words and unpleasant feelings, but God was present to direct, control and save from disruption to his name be the praise. Although seven were licensed to preach, six withdrew. Since that time three of the number have passed to their final reward, and so far as we are able to judge without gathering a single sheaf for the garner above. One after preaching a few years left the country in disgrace. The other two are yet preaching in a sister denomination, but with no more honor or success than they had attained in the church of their early choice. 1,634 members received, present number 6,926; collected for missions $2,611.31. Total for all purposes $33,904.03.

The thirty-eighth annual session of the conference was held by Bishop Glossbrenner, at Marion commencing September 8, 1870. At this conference D. D Hart and G. Ridley were licensed to preach, and D. F. Cender and J. A. Crayton were received on their transfers. Bro. Hart became one of our most successful revivalists. After seven years of successful labor in this conference, he was advised by physicians, on account of failing health to visit the coast, but his zeal for the cause of his Divine Master would not allow him to remain idle long while so many were unsaved. He soon found a place to work, the Sacramento charge being without a preacher he accepted the charge, and while engaged in a revival meeting took hemorrhage of the lungs, and in the midst of the battle for souls, fell pierced by the arrow of death. He expired in his own pulpit, having on the armour he entered the Golden Gate to wear the Victor's Crown. How mysterious are the ways of Providence in removing such efficient men in the midst of their years and usefulness, but when the mists shall all have been cleared away, we shall see the wisdom of God in all his dealings towards his creatures. Faith's anchorage is found in that blessed promise of Christ. "What thou knowest not now, thou shalt know hereafter." On calling the name of J. Davis it was stated that he had gone from labor to reward during the past year. He was one of the oldest members of the conference, (78) having joined at its first session. His love for the church knew no bounds and no sacrifice was too great for him to make, to enlarge her borders and build up her waste places. He labored many years as traveling preacher and much of the time as Presiding Elder. He traveled on horse-back from Crawford Co. Ohio, to Allen Co. Indiana, four times a year, year after year. The roads were very bad, but he seldom missed an appointment, never complained and always wore a smile as he entered the cabins of the West, his salary ranging from seventy-five to one hundred and fifty dollars per year.

He was somewhat eccentric but, a man of clear christian experience, and of unquestioned piety. When he came down to deaths dark waters he found the boatmen waiting to row him over to the other shore. He held the names of his brethren in sweet remembrance in death, and sent to them the following message: "Say to my brethren it is well with me." In accordance with his expressed wishes a funeral sermon was preached in the presence of the conference. Rev. A. Biddle was selected to preach the

> "Servant of God well done,
>   Thy glorious warfares past;
> The battle's fought, the race is won,
> And thou are crowned at last."

M. Errett having also died, the conference requested that Brother Biddle in his sermon on the death of Father Davis, made some suitable remarks on the death of Father Errett he was nearly ninety years of age. One of the most enjoyable events of the conference was the singing on Sabbath afternoon. Your Mission, by a man who has charmed both this country and Europe, by his sacred songs, PHILIP PHILLIPS. The effect produced could not be described. Every christian heart was brought closer to God and to heaven. The conference reported a decrease in membership of 248, and an increase for missions of $329.11.

The following report was adopted by the conference:

ON EDUCATION.

We your Committee on Education, present the following:

Whereas, The marvelous development of the material interests of our country, the restless energy of our people, our perfection in political economy, and the place we occupy in the eyes of the world, all imperatively demand that we should do our part as a church in sending forth among the people, as teachers, men of refinement and education; and,

Whereas, We realize the fact that the times are upon us that unless we carefully foster, and in a sacrificing way lay hold of this department of the interests of the church, our power for good will be materially lessened, our influence as a church crippled, and our respect for ourselves lost; therefore, we are glad to record that feeling which is happily growing, and shows itself in the following expressions from the people: "Give us a strong man;" "Give us men who are able to stand favorably alongside the ministers of other churches—men who, by the depth of their piety and learning, may be able to meet successfully the varied forms of skepticism and infidelity which are constantly pressed upon the minds of the people."

Resolved 1. That we hereby express our gratitude to Almighty God for the success he has vouchsafed to the various institutions of learning under the care of our church, and earnestly pray that while the foundations of the new college-building are being laid deep in the earth, at Westerville, the conviction may grow deeper in the hearts of the ministry and people of the absolute necessity of an educated ministry, if we would meet the wants of the age, and perform our mission as a church.

2. That while we have been deeply pained at the burning of Otterbein University, we are now glad to chronicle the fact of the hopeful state of the interests of that institution, and would earnestly beseech our heavenly Father to spare the lives of those men who, by their tact, energy, and prudence, have thus far placed it on the highway of success.

3. That we as members of the Sandusky Conference, consider Otterbein University worthy of our patronage, and will do all we can to increase its power for good.

4. We also give our unqualified approval to, and promise our hearty co-operation in, the project now on foot for the establishment of a biblical institution, at Dayton, Ohio, to supply a crying need of our church, which grows louder and stronger in the ratio that our responsibilities as a church are felt and our duty to the world known.

R. K. WYANT,
T. J. HARBAUGH, } Committee.
W. MARTIN.

The next conference was held at Winter's Station,

Sandusky Co, Sept. 6, 1871, J. J. Glossbrenner presiding bishop. E. B. Maurer, S. H. Tussing and J. F. Swaney were admitted to membership. Brother Flickinger our Missionary Secretary being present made some remarks in regard to our African mission and that one of its greatest wants was a new row boat to enable our missionaries there to travel from the town of Shengay to Freetown, and other towns. He being asked what it would cost, stated that the expense would be about $200.00. In a very short time $249 00 was secured and the boat was called Sandusky in honor of the conference that furnished the means to buy it. The voluntary contributions of this conference amounted to nearly $800.00 three-fourths of which, or more was paid by ministers and their families setting an example that ought to be followed by their more wealthy brethren.

The conference held its next session in Fostoria, Seneca County, September 4, 1872, and was opened by Bishop Glossbrenner with the usual devotional exercises. The following brethren after examination were licensed to preach; W. W. McCurdy, B. Webb, J. M. Crim; and J. W. Waggoner by transfer.

The following is the report on missions:

The committee on the interests of missions made their report, which was received and adopted:

Your Committee on Missions present the 'following report:

First. We are gratified to state that the amount assessed one year ago has been raised and reported to the chart.

Second. In addition to this there was contributed to the Shengay chapel fund about $125 by the ministers and members of the Sandusky conference.

Believing that there is ability among our people to increase their contributions to the cause of missions as rapidly in the next as they have in the past score of years, and that the wants of the Home, Frontier, and Foreign Missionary Society of our Church demands that such progress should be made; therefore,

Resolved, 1. That we will, by the use of all the means within our reach, especially by preaching, prayer, and paying ourselves, and circulating missionary intelligence, labor to increase the interest and the contributions of our people in behalf of missions.

2. We will also seek to present the claims of missions to our respective congregations at the most suitable time we can select, and at as early a time within the year as it is practicable, and will spare no pains to bring before all the members of the Church their duty to give to this cause according to their ability.

3. We rejoice in the continued prosperity of our mission in Africa, and assure the Board and our missionaries in that field that they shall have our hearty co-operation in carrying forward that mission.

4. We recommend that the basis of assessment for next year be $4,000.

The forty-first session of the conference was held at Osceola, Crawford Co., September 3rd, 1873, with Bishop Weaver in the chair. It was found on calling the roll that four of its number, Wm. Jones, J. Struble, D. G. Ogden and H. G. Spaythe, had been called away during the past year. A special committee was appointed to whom the names of these dear brethren were referred, who made the following report.

We your committee on memoirs beg leave to report the following in reference to our beloved brethren and fathers in the ministry, who have been removed by death from among us, during the past conference year:

I. With reference to John Struble, who fell asleep in Jesus, November 6th, 1872.

II. In reference to Wm. Jones, who departed, February, 1873.

III. In reference to D. G. Ogden, who died, May 29th, 1873.

IV. Also; this conference, since the commencement of its present session, has learned, with deep regret of the death of Father Spaythe, who departed to be with Christ, September 2d, 1873.

Resolved, 1. That in the death of these brethren, we recognize the hand of our Father in Heaven, who doeth all things well.

2. That in the removal, by death, of these ministers of the Sandusky Annual Conference, it is deprived of the example of the good and great, and of the counsel of the wise, matured by many year's experience.

3. That we deeply sympathize with the bereaved families of the above named brethren, and pledge them our sympathy and prayers.

4. That the secretary of this conference send a copy of the above resolutions, respectively to the families of the deceased.

5. That one hour, to-morrow morning, from 10:30 to 11:30 o'clock, be devoted to remarks, on the death of the above named brethren, by members of this conference. And we name for these several services the following brethren, namely:

In the case of Wm. Jones, M. Long.
In the case of John Struble, D. S. Caldwell.
In the case of D. G. Ogden, Wm. Mathers.
In the case of H. G. Spaythe, A. Biddle.

J. BEVER,
M. LONG, } Committee.
M. BULGER,

At the appointed time appropriate remarks were made by the brethren designated, after which the conference passed upon the names of the deceased brethren by a standing vote, and with bowed heads.

The following members were added to the conference, M. A. Powers, J. W. Powell, J. Coup, P.

Warner, and R. Trask; J. B. Resler and W. W. Knipple on their transfers.

The year 1874 was recognized as our Centenary year, and the bishops had arrangements, to make it a year of ingathering of money for the different interests of the church, the conference appointed a committee to arrange the time, and objects for which these collections be taken. The following is their report:

We, your Committee on Centenary interests, would respectfully present the following preamble:

According to the recognized history of our church the year 1874 is recognized as the centenary year of our church—1774 being the year in which the first independent congregation was formed in Baltimore by Rev. Wm. Otterbein and the officers of his congregation. Our heavenly father has granted unto us substantial prosperity in the century of our past history. Our church is being represented among the busy throngs of the east, and holding up the standard of the cross to the peculiar civilization of our western coast Therefore the place we occupy as a church in this land of prosperity, our duty as Americans and our honor as christians belonging to Sandusky Conference, it behooves us to so honor our centenary year that the foundations we now lay may be looked upon with gratitude and honest pride by those who shall crowd our streets, till our farms, and commune at our altars a hundred years to come. The intelligent and successful action of some of our sister churches, our duty to ourselves and the world around us all conspire in this critical year of our church life to urge upon us such course of action as will aim at the strengthening of the walls of Zion and redound to the glory of God.

We would now call your attention to the course of action recommended by our Board of Bishops:

1. That there be a centenary meeting held in every society throughout the church between the 1st of January, 1874, and the 1st of January, 1875, and that at these meetings collections be taken up as thank offerings.

2. That the funds thus secured be equally divided between the Missionary Society, the endowment fund of Union Biblical Seminary, and the Church Erection Society, except when otherwise directed by the donors.

3. As it is necessary for success that there be a uniform plan in this work, we recommend that each minister in charge of a field of labor deliver one or more discourses on the rise, progress, and genius of our church government in every organized society.

4. That special centenary meetings be held at such places as the respective quarterly conferences may direct; the preacher getting all the help he can from every source, and that these meetings be held, if at all practicable, in the months of January and February, 1874.

5. That we make this centenary year a year of prayer, war and sacrifice for the special advancement of the three great interests named by the bishops.

6. That this conference appoint a sub-treasurer to receive all moneys thus raised and transmit it to the general treasurer, except the amount used for local purposes, which is also to be reported to the general treasurer, Rev. D. Berger, Dayton, Ohio.

T. J. HARBAUGH, } Committe.
R. FRENCH,

The report of the committee on resolutions is inserted here, showing the position of the church upon the great moral questions of the day, which is agitating the public mind:

RESOLUTIONS.

The Committee on Resolutions made their report, which was adopted.

We, your Committee on Resolutions, report as follows:

We believe that, as ministers of the gospel of Christ and stewards of the manifold grace of God, it becomes us in all things to be ensamples of the flock.

1. In seeking for the great fullness of salvation from sin.

2. In abstaining from every appearance of evil. Therefore,

Resolved, 1. That we now reconsecrate ourselves to the service of God and the great work of the ministery, humbling ourselves under the mighty hand of God, deploring our past unfaithfulness, and humbly seeking grace for time to come.

2. That in view of the growing evils of the time, we set our faces and raise our voices against,

1. Intemperance in all its forms, including the use, as a beverage, of all intoxicating drinks, vinous, distilled, or fermented. The use of tobacco in any form, as a gratification of vitiated appetite, and the immoderate use of things that are good.

2. Sabbath desecration in doing labor on the Lord's day; in social visiting, and in attending meetings for mental culture and social entertainment without regard to religion.

3. Laciviousness, by which the mighty have fallen, and innumerable evils have been entailed upon own fallen race.

The next conference was held at Westerville, Franklin Co., September 16th, 1874. J. Weaver was presiding bishop. This was outside the bounds of the conference, but being the seat of OTTERBEIN UNIVERSITY, and SANDUSKY being one of the co-operating conferences, it was thought by holding its session under the shadow of this institution of learning, it would bring the conference into closer sympathy with the school, and thus secure it friends and students. So by special request of the citizens of Westerville this session was held there, which proved in the main to be a pleasant and harmonious one;

not only satisfactory to the conference itself, but to those that entertained as well. The following members were received: H. F. Hartzell, H. L. Downing, W. C. Meek and I. H Green. A. Orr was received on his transfer and A. J. Klingle from the M. E. Church.

The committee to whom our centenary interests was committed made their report, which was amended and adopted as follows:

CENTENARY COMMITTEE'S REPORT.

Whereas, In the providence of God it has been our good fortune to have our existence in the world, and in this the church of our choice, at the period of the termination of the first hundred years of its existence; and,

Whereas, The history of this church has been signalized through all the past by the most unmistakable demonstrations of the divine presence, in the success that has characterized all its efforts from its infancy, under the fostering care of its founders and their successors, down to the present; therefore,

Resolved, 1. That we deem it to be our highest as well as our most pleasant duty and privilege to express to our kind and beneficent heavenly Father a tribute of gratitude, corresponding as nearly as may be, to the numerous blessings that we as a church have, under God, enjoyed through all these years.

2. That while other churches, which have been less careful in guarding the purity and sancity of their altars, have far outstripped us in the race to popular fame and numerical strength, yet, we though somewhat slow, have made sure and steady progress in all the christian and moral reforms that have distinguished the general church of America.

3. That while our position as a church in relation to American slavery retarded our seeming prosperity in the slave states for many years, yet an infinitely wise God sustained us all through this fiery ordeal to which our antislavery antecedents had subjected us, till in God's own time he has seen fit to vindicate his own justice and the righteousness of our legislation on this question, until now in this regard our principles are indorsed by the legislative enactments of this great nation, and approval by the universal sanction of all truly civil and christian powers to earth.

4. That we attribute our success in the various reforms of the past and present to the fact that our legislation on these questions has been prohibitory, thereby guarding the very portals against any encroachments into our communion and fellowship by unworthy and designing persons.

5. That we would recommend, in view of the financial crisis that to a great extent interferes with our desired success in our centenary collections, that these efforts be continued *for two years* instead

of one—thereby hoping to realize an amount for various enterprises of the Church worthy the name of a centenary offering.

6. That we would urge upon our ministers and all concerned to continued and special efforts during the entire year of 1874, to raise centenary funds for the purposes recommended by the late General Conference, and that this conference appoint some one available for each district, who can take hold of this work, and hold centenary-meetings, in co-operation with the preachers on their respective fields, for said purposes, between now and January 1st, 1875, and thereafter the preachers continue, in private and public, to work on in this cause, as per fifth item in this report.

7. That the presiding elders take the oversight of these meetings, make appointments, and secure suitable persons to attend them.

8. That Otterbein University be recognized as one of the chief objects of centenary benevolence in connection with the interests designated by the General Conference.

D. S. CALDWELL,
L. MOORE,   } Committee.
T. J. HARBAUGH,

An increase of 274 members reported over last year's report whole number 7,124, collected for missions $3,358.000 a decrease of $123.00; collected for all purposes $49,070.76.

The conference met in its forty-third session, in Galion, Crawford Co., September 8th, 1875. The presiding bishop J. Weaver opened the conference with the usual religious services. The following applicants were licensed to preach: J. Paul, C. L. Bevington, H. C. Bevington, J. J. Strohl, N. S. Long, I. Freeze and L. Sharp; B. B. Beebe was received on transfer, and B. M. Long from the Congregational Church.

The missionary and educational work received special attention by speeches and resolutions to give greater efficiency to these factors of the church to lead the masses to better, happier and more useful lives. Dr. Thompson, of Otterbein University, delivered an address on religious education that was highly appreciated by all who heard it; Rev. J. B. Resler spoke in behalf of Union Biblical Seminary and secured on the conference floor the amount of $240.00 to aid in the purchase of a library.

In 1876 the conference convened in Findlay, Hancock Co., September 6th, with Bishop Weaver in the chair. At this conference the subject of establishing an institution of learning within its bounds was discussed. A board of trustees was appointed, with instructions to locate and open such an institution as soon as sufficient money could be secured. These preliminary steps soon led to the founding of FOSTORIA ACADEMY. This institution has been in operation nearly eight years, and has had as fine a class of young men and ladies as ever filled the halls of any institution of learning, who have been an honor to the school and a blessing to the church, and were it not for the heavy debt that like a millstone hangs about its neck would prove in the years to come a greater blessing than it has in the years that are past. Who will lift this heavy burden from its shoulders and place it upon a plane of greater usefulness? It must be done soon or the opportunity will have passed forever.

BISHOP EDWARDS having died during the year memorial services were held by the conference as a small tribute of respect to him who had so often presided over its deliberations. Touching remarks were made by Bishop Weaver and others on the life and labors, and triumphant death of this faithful servant of God. The committee on memoirs made the following report:

REPORT OF COMMITTEE ON MEMOIRS.

Resolved, 1. That we hereby express our appreciation of the life and labors of our late lamented bishop, David Edwards, D. D., and would bow submissively to the divine Providence removing him from our midst.

2. That we remember with satisfaction the admirable qualities in his character of honest industry,

unvaried frankness, uniform integrity in all the relations of life, as worthy of emulation.

3. That we feel with keenness the loss and vacancy occasioned by his death, but will still seek to profit by his admonitions, counsels, reproofs, sound bible teaching, and examplary life.

4. That we condole with the family of the deceased, and the friends in the church generally, in the severe loss, and pray God that the especial tenderness, devotion, and constancy in the decline of his life may sweetly insinuate itself into all our hearts and be a controlling element in our lives, and that as he could not live longer to preach salvation by faith in Christ, we, who yet live, will take up the devout message with more earnestness, if possible, than ever in the past.

5. That we will seek to embalm his memory by endeavoring to endow a scholarship of $5,000.00 in Otterbein University, to be under the control of the faculty of said college, for the education of worthy young men for the ministry of Christ.

6. That we suggest to our publishing agent the propriety of issuing from our office—in our Sabbath School library—the life of Bishop Edwards.

Rev. William Clippinger was born in Salem, Montgomery Co., Ohio, April 17, 1841. He was converted to God at about eighteen years of age, in Bellfontaine, under the ministerial labors of Rev. Mr. Parker. He came with his parents to Ottawa—as nearly as we know—in 1860. He attended Otterbein University over two years. During this time he was held in high esteem for his piety, social qualities, and faithfulness as a student. Let his example in the culture of his mind be followed by others. Education with grace is a source of much power for good.

Bro. Clippinger married the estimable daughter—Mary Malinda—of that pioneer of the United Brethren in Christ, in Putnam Co., Ohio, Wm. Galbreath, July 19, 1865. Two years before this, in 1863, he received license to preach the gospel of Christ, under the eldership of Rev. M. Bulger. He joined the annual conference in 1864, entered the itinerancy in 1866, and was ordained to the office of elder in 1873, Bishop Weaver presiding. He traveled on Bucyrus Circuit part of one year; on Powell's Creek Circuit, and on Beaver Creek Circuit, where failing health obliged him to cease the work. He was by profession a teacher, and after entering the ministry part of his time was spent in this calling. He stood among the foremost Sabbath School workers in the conference, and was a leading spirit in this work in his own county. As an itinerant he was faithful and industrious, and gave promise of large usefulness. He died after a lingering illness of over one year, at his own home in Ottawa, Putnam County, Ohio, in the triumphs of a Christian faith, April 22, A. D. 1876, aged 34 years, 11 months and 25 days, the funeral services being conducted by Rev. T. J. Harlaugh. He was plain and argumentative in his preaching, industrious and faithful in his pastoral work, looked carefully after the general interest of the church, and was becoming more and more earnest and pathetic in his pulpit ministrations.

We condole with the family and friends of the deceased, and as a conference remember Brother Clippinger with kindness, bowing in submission to the divine will. Respectfully submitted.

By the Committtee,
{ W. MARTIN.
DANIEL GLANCY.
JNO. V. POTTS.

The following report on Missions is worthy a place here:

REPORT OF COMMITTEE ON MISSIONS.

When we look at the moral condition of the inhabitants of earth, consisting as they do of about fourteen hundred million souls redeemed by the blood of Christ, we will find that probably not over three hundred and fifty or four hundred millions bear the name of christian. Many of *those* bear that hallowed name in vain, being confirmed in unbelief, or are the slaves of sinful lust or habits.

Probably not over fifty millions seen by the inscrutable eye of God are seen in salvation's ark.

Many of those who are without, are sunken in their filthy and vicious habits beyond the power of human language to describe; and,

Whereas, God has indicated his will by prophecy, promise, and parable, that they should be illuminated and saved; and,

Whereas, He has thrown this evangelizing work directly upon his church in such a way that to refuse to do it is to forfeit the christian name, and also become stained with the blood of our brethren; therefore,

Resolved, 1. That we will push forward our missionary work, both domestic and foreign, with unremitting zeal, striving to bring out all the unemployed resources of the church by talking on this subject in the family circles which we enter, and on all other suitable occcasions.

2. That we will solicit annual contributions from all our people after an earnest and forcible public presentation of its claims.

3. That we are highly gratified with the success which has attended our foreign missions. Especially do we most heartily approve of the effort to establish an industrial school in connection with our African mission; and we most heartily pledge them our sympathy and co-operation.

J. A. CRAYTON.

The following brethren were received into the conference: J. E. Hill, J Aumiller, A. J. Nichols, and G. P. Macklin; O. H. Ramsey was received from the M. E. Church.

The conference held its next session at Fostoria, Seneca Co., commencing September 12th, 1877, Bishop Dixon presiding. This conference was perhaps the most largely attended of any one ever held; 94 being present and only 10 absent. The following applicants were licensed to preach: M. E. Spahr, M. Dewitt Long, I. P. Lea, Z. Kirk, J. W. Eastman, J. W. Myers and D. O. Tussing. The general conference having passed a law at its late session authorizing the annual conferences to adopt lay delegation when two-thirds so desired it, the subject was taken up, but in view of a contemplated division of the conference, the matter was laid over for one year. Death had again invaded our ranks, and the announcement was made that S. Essex, one of our most efficient itinerants had gone to rest. The following paper was adopted:

MEMOIR OF REV. SAMUEL ESSEX.

In the afflictive dispensations of divine Providence we, as a conference, are again called to mourn. Rev. Samuel Essex fell asleep in Jesus, April 11, 1877, aged 59 years, 4 months, and 15 days. His labors in the ministery of the gospel embraced twenty-three years. His record on the various fields he traveled shows that his was a successful itinerant life. Though not obtrusive in his manner of work yet he aimed to be vigilent and careful in the work of saving souls. That work was cut short by the hand of Death, perhaps only to human sight; but his example and influence will live on, and tell in the records of the now unfolding future. His faith was firm to the end; and a frequent expression in his last affliction was, "I am as firm as a rock." He often referred to his exclusive trust in the attonement made by the blood of Christ. He has gone but a little before the rest of us. Now realizing what "eye hath not seen nor ear heard," he would no doubt say to us, "Be faithful," and becken us up to enjoy the glory of the redeemed. Let us labor and wait a little while, and then realize what he has entered upon.

> A. Rose,
> D. Glancy,   } Committee.
> T. J. Harbaugh.

The conference for 1878 was held in Vanlue, Hancock Co., August 28th. J. Dixon the presiding bishop opened the conference by the useful services. At this conference that part lying south of the Pittsburg & Fort Wayne railroad was taken off according to an act of the General Conference, taking twenty ministers and 1,113 members, reducing our membership from 7,961 to 6,748 and ministerial force from 104 to 84. Death having removed since our last meeting H. C. Bevington, A. Spracklin and

D. Glancy. The following committee on memoirs was appointed: J. French, J. Bever and M. Long who made the following report:

Whereas, In the Providence of our Heavenly Father, three of our ministerial brethren, viz, Alfred Spracklin, Daniel Glancy and H. C. Bevington have been removed by death during the past conference year. Therefore,

Resolved, 1. That while we meekly bow to the divine will in taking these brethren from labor to reward, we deeply feel the loss in their removal both in the conference and in the church, and we sincerely express our deep sorrow by pouring out our sympathies and mingling our tears with the afflicted and grief stricken hearts of their bereaved families.

Resolved, 2. That a copy of this report be forwarded to the "Telescope" office for publication. We recommend that the hour of three o'clock P. M. to-day be set apart by this conference to make honorable mention of these beloved departed brethren and that brethren be requested to deliver addresses on their lives, labors and death, viz: on A. Spracklin, A. Biddle; D. Glancy, T. J. Harbaugh; on H. C. Bevington, L. Moore.

Brother Glancy had been a member of the conference thirty-three years. He was strongly attached to his church; sound in theology, and a christian in the broadest sense of that term. Brother Bevington had just commenced upon a career of usefulness, and why he should be cut down in the morning of life, must remain to us a mystery, until revealed by Him who doeth all things according to his own will. The following brethren were licensed to preach: S. H. Brake, R. Fought, J. Walker and J. Sargent.

Bishop Dixon held the next session of the conference at Columbus Grove, Putnam County, commencing September 10th, 1879. The following applicants after examination were admitted to membership in the conference: J. A. Young, W. H. Evans, C. H. Lemmon, M. H. Tussing, J. P. Rigg, J. E. Husted, A. B. Leonard, J. Kirk and T. C. McCurdy; E. A. Starkey was received on his transfer. Nothing of special interest out of the usual order of business was transacted at this conference. The missionary, and educational work of the conference was carefully looked after, and such action taken as it was believed would best advance these important interests of the church. The woman's work was fully recognized by the conference, and expressions of encouragement and help proffered by the passage of the following resolution: "We thank God that the women of this church, engaged in the missionary work in an organized form, and are having a good degree of success; and we pledge our sympathy and encouragement in the good work in which they are engaged, and will render them all the assistance we can consistently with our other duties." On Saturday evening the claims of the Woman's

Missionary Society were presented by Mrs. Emeline Day, Mrs. Emeline Bender and others after which a collection was taken of $18 22 for the erection of a mission house in Africa under the care of the Woman's Missionary Society of this church.

On the 8th day of September 1880, the conference convened at Rising Sun, Wood Co., and was opened by Bishop Dixon reading the scriptures, singing and prayer. The following applicants after examination were licensed to preach the gospel: M. M. Marshall, R. Trask, H. Doty, J. W. Hipple, G. W. Welty, S. Hall and I. L. Miller.

The committee on memoirs reported as follows. The report was adopted:

REPORT OF COMMITTEE ON MEMOIRS.

John Bell was born July 2, 1809, in Belmont Co., Ohio. He was soundly converted to God in his sixteenth year, and maintained his Christian integrity until his death, which occurred October 14, 1879; his age being 70 years, 3 months and 7 days.

Soon after his conversion he felt divinely impressed to preach the gospel. He was then a member of the Methodist Episcopal Church, and they gave him authority to preach. His labors were wonderfully blessed. During the slavery agitation of those days he felt it his duty to join the Wesleyan Church, and was an itinerant in that body for twenty years; and did much to educate the public conscience on the great crime of human slavery.

Ffteen years ago he united with the Sandusky Annual Conference, but he remained in a local relation in the ministry, his age and infirmities forbidding his entering the regular work.

As a citizen he was a patriot; as a man, dignified; as a husband and father, filling the Scripture model; as a friend, fast and true. In character he was of the positive type, and had clear conceptions of truths and doctrines. The Bible was his standard for fifty years. He was on the alter of consecration, and cultivated a conscience void of offense toward God and man. Among his last words were, "I am in peace with God and with all men." His victory over the last enemy was most signal and triumphant. He leaves a wife and seven children, and also many friends, who expect to meet him in the better land.

Rev. R. K. Wyant died Aug. 23, on his work on Hamler Mission. He preached on Saturday night, and on Sabbath twice. He stayed over night at Bro. Young's, and was not able to leave the place again. On the next Friday he died. For forty-eight hours, during his illness, he was speechless, but before he died his speech returned. From that time until he died he praised the Lord. His last words were, "Praise His holy name, He has come!" He was buried at Kansas, on the 24th, Bro. Ramsey preaching the funeral sermon.

Bro. Wyant joined our conference at Fostoria some years ago, and had long felt it his duty to preach the gospel. He was a man of wonderful tenacity of purpose, and in his youth, even amidst neglect and discouragement, became a fair scholar. As a minister in this conference he did its bidding without murmuring, going upon barren fields, consulting only his duty, and humbly holding forth the word of life. He was a man of principle and conscience, and many and great sacrifices were made by him to fulfill what he felt to be the direction of his heavenly Father, and his last preaching was with unction and power.

With reference to the names of Wm. Miller and Fought, we can write nothing on account of lack of information.

Rev. W. McDowell, an aged minister of this conference, who died during this conference year, was born in Scotland, and reared in the Covenanter Church. He came to this country and located in Wyandotte County, Ohio, in about the year 1834, and joined our church soon after. He sustained a local relation as a minister for over forty years. He died in peace at the residence of his daughter in Mt. Blanchard, Ohio.

Bro. McDowell was a man of great energy and native force of character, a leader of men. He was an ardent lover of God's word, and a giant in defense of Christian doctrine. He highly prized his relationship to the ministerial brethren, and was practically interested in all the varied forms of our church work.

Resolved, In consideration of the death of these dear brethren, that we extend our sympathy to the sorrowing friends of these men who have fallen from our ranks here and joined the other part of the family on the other side of the river.

Resolved, That we will prayerfully consider our own frailty and the faithfulness of our heavenly Father in the keeping of his precious promises.

T. J. HARBAUGH,
L. MOORE, } Committee.
D. R. MILLER.

REPORT OF COMMITTEE ON RESOLUTIONS.

We, your committee on resolutions, beg leave to report as follows:

Resolved, That it shall be our aim to enlarge the borders of our Zion, build up the waste places, and strengthen all our churches by every laudable means in our power; and try more than ever to utilize all our forces, that our churches may become numerous, permanent and strong, furnishing places for every approved worker in the vineyard.

Resolved, That we earnestly advise all persons called of God to the ministry, to thoroughly qualify themselves for the sacred work, either by private study, or a course at Otterbein University, Union Biblical Seminary, or Fostoria Academy.

Resolved, That we hereby pledge to each other fidelity to our own principles and historic life; that we will not needlessly try to mend or trifle with our organic form as a christian body, and that we can not hope to permanently succeed nor fully accomplish our missions in opposition to our own recognized principle and policy, and that whatever success may attend us in diverging lines of thought is but ficticious, temporary and dangerous.

Resolved, That the Chair be instructed to appoint a committee of three on statistics, who shall meet one half day in advance of the conference session and receive the reports from the preachers, record the same in regular order for conference use, and report the same at the opening of the conference.

Resolved, That the preachers of this conference be required, if they cannot be present at the time specified in the above resolution, to send a correct statement of the statistics required.

Resolved, That the practice of many of our fields of labor in paying to their ministers less than they agree, is a crying evil, which we sincerely condemn as a grievous wrong, to be carefully avoided in the future.

Resolved, That this conference gives its unqualified disapproval to the practice of some who withhold their quarterage on account of disagreement with the pastor in charge, there being ample provisions for obtaining justice.

Resolved, that we set ourselves in opposition to all Sunday excursions, that our people be earnestly entreated to refrain from them, as being a sin against God and society; that we also condemn any method of proceeding at any time whereby the people are led into infidelity.

Resolved, That we consider intemperance arising from intoxicants, narcotics, and sensuality as the crowning and crying sin of our age, and that the laws of our church in this regard should be vigorously enforced.

Resolved, That in view of the cordial reception, christian courtesies, and kind entertainment of the conference by the people of Rising Sun, we hereby tender to them our sincere thanks, and pray that the spirit of God may abide with them forever.

D. S. CALDWELL.

The forty-ninth session of the conference was held in Sycamore, Wyandotte County, September 21st, 1881, and was opened by Bishop Glossbrenner by the usual services. At this time the nation was draped in mourning for the loss of her chief magistrate, James A. Garfield, whose death was caused by the bullet of a cruel assassin The conference appointed a committee to draft resolutions, expressive of the feelings of the conference, in this, the time of the nation's grief; the following report was adopted:

REPORT ON THE DEATH OF THE PRESIDENT OF THE UNITED STATES.

Whereas, The Supreme Ruler of Nations has suffered the blow of an assassin to cause the death of James A. Garfield, President of the United States, Therefore,

Resolved, 1. That in this act of the assassin is manifest the evil fruit of the increasing unkind, false and malicious assaults upon the character and acts of the country's public servant, and those who are brought before the people for positions of honor and trust.

2. That in the death of President Garfield, the nation suffers the loss of a public servant, distinguished for scholastic ability, intelligence, pure and able statesmanship, and Ohio one of its brightest stars

3. That the church has lost a noble public example of piety, humility and devotion to our holy christianity.

4. That while we would not attempt the interpretation of this afflicting providence, we with satisfaction recognize the truth so heroically and pertinently uttered by our now deceased President on receiving the news of the assassination of the lamented Lincoln, viz.: that "GOD REIGNS; and

though the Chief of the nation is dead the government at Washington still lives."

5. That we tender to the bereaved family of the deceased our heartfelt sympathy and pledge them our prayers.

6. That a copy of these resolutions be forwarded to the widow of the deceased.

Respectfully,

D. R. Miller. ⎫
M. Bulger. ⎬ Committee.
J. W. Eastman. ⎭

Again the conference was called upon to pass up on the names of three of its number who had been called to join the army on the other shore. A committee on memoirs was appointed who made the following report:

Rev. Alvin Rose, was born in Concord Township, Delaware County, O., Nov. 1st, 1827. He died at his home in Findlay, Hancock Co. O., September 6th, 1881, at the age of fifty-three years ten months and five days. Being early left an orphan, he was cared for by an aunt until he reached the age of fourteen years. From that time he was compelled to rely upon his own exertions for a livelihood. During this period of his life he endured many hardships with a fortitude and patience which fitted him for the eventful career which followed. He early received religious impressions which were deep and lasting. But he did not become a subject of regenerating grace until he arrived at manhood. In the year 1858 he commenced his ministerial work, receiving his first license at the hands of Rev. A. Biddle. The year following he joined the Sandusky Conference of the United Brethren Church, from that time until his death he was never without a field of labor from the church. As pastor he officiated first upon his home circuit, afterward upon the following circuits of this conference: Flat Rock, Findlay, Van Buren, Carey, Tawa and Salem. He served seven years as Presiding Elder, which office he held at the time of his death. He was four times elected to represent his conference in the General Conference of the Church, the last time being unable to attend because of the sickness which resulted in his death. At the time of his death he was a member of the board of trustees of Fostora Academy and of Otterbein University. In all the positions to which he was called by the voice of his brethren he never betrayed their trust. He was a man of firm convictions of right, bold and outspoken in the expression of his sentiments and unflinching in his determination to do his duty.

The last year of his life was one of great physical suffering, that terrible, fatal disease, consumption was slowly but surely bearing him to the tomb. At first it was very hard for him to consent to be taken away from his family, his church and the work of his Divine Master in the prime of life, and at a time when his services were so much needed. The fact disturbed the tranquility of his spirit for a time, but as the days and months passed away, he settled into a calm unwavering trust, in the goodness and wisdom of God's providence.

His last hours were hours of struggle and triumph. Shortly before his death he remarked to his wife "Now I am in the valley, but not through yet," in a few moments a bright, happy expression overspread his features, and uplifting his hands, he said, "It is all bright now! It is all glory! glory! glory!" Then he sank into an unconscious state and softly, gently and peacefully his spirit was borne to the bosom of the Eternal Father. Thus passed away a man whose grandest monument, than which none can be grander is the testimony of all who knew him. "He was a good man."

Rev. F. N. Clymer, of Sandusky Annual Conference was converted many years ago at a camp meeting held by the United Brethren in Fairfield County, O., and united with the church. He moved to Hancock County and joined the church on Tawa Circuit. This Circuit gave him a quarterly conference license to preach the gospel and recommended him to the Annual Conference, where he was received and licensed.

Bro. Clymer was a good man and always ready for work when duty called him. He died in great peace in January, 1881.

Rev. T. J. McCurdy united with the United Brethren Church on Bucyrus Circuit.

He received quarterly conference license to preach from the same Circuit in the autumn of 1876, when L. Moore was pastor, and A. Rose presiding elder. After this he moved to Flat Rock Circuit. In September, 1879, his Circuit recommended him to the Annual Conference which met at Columbus Grove where he was licensed to preach by the Annual Conference, and went to Ottawa Station. The conference at Rising Sun sent him to Dupont, where he was engaged in his Master's employ when death met and claimed him—April 11, 1881, aged about thirty years.

Brother McCurdy followed teaching as a profession for several years before he entered the ministry. He was a young man of fair promise. His call was very sudden, but there is no doubt he was prepared for the summons.

In view of the departure from our midst of these our brethren and fellow workers, we recommend the adoption of the following resolutions:

1. That, while we deeply feel their loss, we meekly bow to the providence of our God, who doeth all things well, praying him to endow us with his holy spirit that we may imitate their virtues.

2. That we tender to the families of the deceased our heartfelt sympathy, and pray God to comfort their hearts, and sustain them in the midst of the troubles and the responsibilities of this life.

We recommend that W. Martin make some remarks in the case of F. N. Clymer; L. Moore, in the case of T. J. McCurdy; and I. Crouse, A. W. Holden, and E. A. Starkey in the case of A. Rose.

Respectfully submitted,

S. H. RAUDEBAUGH.
L. MOORE. } Committee.
E. A. STARKEY.

The following brethren were admitted to membership: W. J. Easterbrook and C. F. Hill; W. T. Jackson was received on his transfer.

The next conference was held by Bishop Glossbrenner, in North Baltimore, Wood Co., commencing September 13th, 1882. The bishop's sermon on Sabbath, from the text, "Sow Beside all Waters," was one of exceeding beauty and power. He scarcely knew whether he was in the body or out of the body. The holy ghost fell on the congregation somewhat like unto the day of Pentecost. Many thought it would be his last visit to the conference, but God ordered it otherwise; he visited us once more before passing to his eternal rest. We were all so favored with the presence of Brother Gomer, our missionary from Africa, who gave us a fine lecture about the country, customs, and manners of life in Africa, exhibiting articles of idolatry and superstition. He told us of the wonderful influence of the gospel in evangelizing the heathen world, the blessed results already secured, the wide openings before the christian church, and the Macedonian cry, "Come over and help us."

Bro. Gomer's visit to our conference awakened a new interest in the minds of many in regard to our work in Africa, causing them to give more liberally for its support. J. R. Osburn, W. R. Arnold, E. D. Price and W. P. Bender were received into membership in the conference.

The conference held its next session at Helena, Sandusky Co., commencing September 19th, 1883. On the calling of Bishop Glossbrenner's name, the following paper was presented and adopted by a standing vote: In view of the long, extensive, and faithful life of Bishop Glossbrenner in the church of the Lord Jusus Christ, and especially his untiring labors and efforts to build up and extend the interests of the United Brethren Church, as well as his unfaltering loyalty to her polity and peculiarities; therefore,

Resolved, 1. That we hereby express our heartfelt gratitude to our heavenly father in permitting him once more to visit this cenference in his official capacity.

2. That in adopting this paper we hereby express our entire satisfaction with his official labors as far as known to us, and especially in this conference.

3. That we will pray that God may continue to give him sufficient health to labor for many more years in the cause of the Master.

The following brethren were received into the conference: G. W. Taylor and G. W. Clymer; J. Park and W. S. Sage on their transfers from Auglaize. Bro. Sage had been converted and licensed to preach in our own conference, but while attending Union Biblical Seminary joined the Auglaize conference as a matter of convenience. He being under appointment as a missionary to Africa, was ordained to the office of an elder in the church, by laying on of hands by the bishop and two elders. Mrs. Sage being under appointment, was also set apart for the missionary work by laying on of hands, as a helper. On calling the name of S. Hall it was stated that he had died within the year. The following paper was adopted by the conference :

REPORT OF COMMITTEE ON MEMOIRS.

The subject of this paper, Rev. Samuel Hall, was born in Westmoreland County, Pa., in the year 1848, June 2d.

He was converted when sixteen years of age and become a member of the M. E. Church, and finally in the year 1879 became a member of the U. B. Church at Honey Creek Chapel. He was received into this conference at Rising Sun, Wood County, O., September, 1880.

He was a man of deep spirituality. His last words to his pastor were, "Tell the people at Harmony that I am still trusting in Jesus." His last words to his wife were, "There is not a shadow in the way." He died peacefully, Dec. 29, 1882.

Resolved, 1. That our loss is his eternal gain, and therefore we submit to the will of Him who is too wise to err and too good to do wrong.

2. That we as a conference extend our sympathies and prayers to his bereaved wife and three children.

3. That a copy of these resolutions be published in the *Religious Telescope*.

That the Rev. L. Moore and his pastor be requested to make remarks.

Respectfully submitted.

N. S. LONG.
S. H. RAUDEBAUGH.

The following excellent report on missions was adopted:

REPORT ON MISSIONS.

The gospel is the power of God unto salvation to every one that believeth. Faith cometh by hearing and hearing by the preaching of the word. The church is the agent through which God would speedily effect the evangalization of the world. The command comes ringing down through the ages from the lips of the blessed Master, "Go work to-day in my vineyard." To the inquiry, where shall we work, his answer is, "The field is the world." We, as a denomination, believe in the divine authority for missionary work; therefore,

Resolved, 1. That we are grateful to our heavenly Father for the success attending our labors thus far.

2. The success attending our efforts in Africa and Germany.

3. The successful trip accomplished by our Secretary, D. K. Flickinger, to Europe and Africa; also the transfer of Mendi Mission and appropriations thereto.

4. We bid Brother Billheimer Godspeed in his mission to England, and hope and pray that he may be successful in his work there.

5. We express our confidence in our missionary Board that they have and will continue to judiciously manage the affairs connected with our missionary work. in appointments and appropriations for the best interests of the cause.

6. We pray our Father in heaven to give grace and faithfulness to the workers in the foreign and frontier fields; and may the presence of the Master

go with Bro. Sage and wife, who have recently been appointed to Africa.

7. We are gratified for the measure of success attending our efforts to liquidate the debt resting upon our missionary society.

8. We advise that the fields which have not reported full in the debt assessment be urged by the preacher to raise the amount as soon as possible.

9. We look with pride upon the continued and increasing success of the Woman's Missionary Society and in every way we can bid them Godspeed.

10. With increasing opportunities, and increasing facilities for work, we will give ourselves to prayer and deeper consecration of the work, believing for a greater baptism of missionary fire and the future success of our several fields of missionary work.

A. B. LEONARD, Committee.

The following reports on resolutions and temperance was adopted:

REPORT OF THE COMMITTEE ON TEMPERANCE.

Whereas, The opportunity of a lifetime has come to the people of the commonwealthh of Ohio, to express their feelings on the traffic in intoxicating liquors; therefore,

Resolved, 1. That we return thanks to the legislature for giving the people of this state an opportunity to vote untrammeled by partisan politics.

2. That we consider the first proposed amendment as unwise, as uncalled for, and as a step backward, and as such unworthy the support of christian and temperance men.

3. That we are in favor of constitutional prohibition, and believe it to be the only effective antidote from the gigantic curse of intemperance arising from the use of intoxicating liquors.

4. That we will support the second or prohibitory amendment, and urge all our people to give it their unwavering support.

5. That we as ministers will not move, if it will prevent us from voting, until after the 9th day of October.

G. P. MACKLIN.
A. B. LEONARD.
N. S. LONG.

REPORT OF COMMITTEE ON RESOLUTIONS.

Resolved, 1. That it is fitting that we return our sincere gratitude to almighty God for the manifestations of his goodness to us during the year that is past, and bestowing his blessing upon us in our special work as embassadors of his; and that we will now covenant anew to apply ourselves more diligently, if possible, to the work committed unto us.

2. That we hail with delight the providential

forecasting of an opportunity to slay within the border of our commonwealth, the monster demon intemperance.

3. That we believe the command, "Speak not evil one of another, brethren," is as binding upon us as it was upon those to whom it was addressed by the apostle; and by its strict observance we may promote the happiness of one another, and advance the interest of the kingdom of our Redeemer.

4. That we take great pleasure in giving expression to our appreciation of the services rendered so excellently and in such strict keeping with the polity of this church, by Bishop Glossbrenner, during the present session of this conference.

5. That we are greatly pleased at the manner in which the citizens of Helena have extended the courtesies and freedom of their homes to the members of and visitors to this conference.

Respectfully submitted,

W. A. KEESY.
J. W. EASTMAN.
E. B. MAURER.

The increase in membership the past year was 104, the whole number being 6851. Missionary money collected $3,011.90.

The next session of the conference was held at Columbus Grove from September 17th to the 22d

1884. Bishop Glossbrenner having been taken sick while on his district, was under the necessity of returning to his home in Virginia. Rev. D. K. Flickinger was elected to preside over the conference, assisted by Rev. D. R. Miller.

In calling the names of certain brethren it was stated they belonged to the Grand Army of the Republic. The conference passed the following resolution by a vote of 57 to 2: "That it is the sense of this conference, that the Grand Army of the Republic is not strictly a secret society and that membership in the same is not by us as a conference, considered to be a violation of our rule on secret societies." M. V. Davis, J. H. Arnold, G. L. Bender, L. T. Hanawalt, M. B. Lanker and D. K. Steiner were licensed to preach. R. Rock, was received on transfer from Muskingum.

The next conference was held by Bishop J. Weaver at Rawson, Hancock County, commencing September 23d, 1885. The Woman's Missionary Society was represented in the conference by sister Jennie Cramer of Bowling Green. She presented their Chinese mission in Portland, Oregon, as a special interest. Bishop Weaver, spoke on woman's work in the cause of mission and especially the good work they are doing on the coast, after which a collection was taken for the benefit of the Portland mission house amounting to $32.84. The following applicants after examination were licensed to preach the gospel: I. E. Barnes, I. E. Ingle, J. P. Marshall, T. H. Sonedecker, and F. E. Fitzwater. Death had once more envaded our ranks, and the name of W. K. Leonard must forever drop from the roll of members. The following report was made and adopted by the conference:

REPORT OF COMMITTEE ON MEMOIRS.

We, your committee on memoirs, respectfully submit the following:

The great enemy and the last to be destroyed, has again invaded the rank and file of the ministery of this conference, and it hath pleased our Heavenly Father to remove from our ranks Rev. W. K. Leonard, who became a member of this conference held at Columbus Grove in 1879, who died June 14, 1885.

Bro. Leonard served but a few years in the ministery, as you know, yet he was permitted to lead quite a number to Christ and unto the church.

He possessed a spirit of perseverance to a large degree, and was a diligent student.

While possessing peculiarities he was large hearted, and from his life there went forth the testimony that Christ lived in him the hope of glory. When nearing the time of his departure he said to a brother minister, "I can say like the sainted Otterbein: 'O, Jesus, I die, but thou livest, and soon I shall live with thee.'"

In his death the conference sustains a loss, yet we are thankful to God; to Brother Leonard it is infinite gain. As a conference we extend to Sister Leonard our sympathies. and pray that the comforter of hearts may sustain her in her severe affliction, and that she may fully trust in him who doeth all things well."

     Respectfully,

       J. FRENCH.
       A. POWELL.
       A. B. LEONARD.

We believe it to be the duty of the conference to remember tenderly those that fall in its ranks, but is not the faithful itinerants wife, who has fallen by his side, in the battle for souls, equally worthy of recognition, so it thought at this session, and passed upon the name of one whose sun went down before it had reached the meridian, being but twenty-seven years of age.

IN AFFECTIONATE MEMORY OF HATTIE BENDER.

Inasmuch as our Heavenly Father has called from labor and suffering to rest, reward an immortal youth, health and unspeakably joy, Hattie, the faithful and affectionate itinerant wife of Rev. W. P. Bender and daughter of Rev. Wm. and Mrs. C. Mathers, and a noble and earnest christian woman and worker of unusual piety, intelligence and efficiency, therefore.

Resolved, 1. The cause of Christ sustains a loss incalculable, and because of this we are sad, but rejoice in her examplary life and her unfaltering faith in Jesus and the gospel from childhood to the end of life's journey and in her triumphant death.

2. That we deeply sympathize with Bro. Bender in the so early loss of his wife and with Bro. and Sister Mathers and her brothers and sisters in their sore bereavement.

3. That these resolutions be recorded in the conference "journal" in affectionate token of our high appreciation of Hattie and all the faithful and sacrificing wives of our itinerants.

R. Rock.
A. B. Leonard.

The following report on temperance was adopted:

REPORT ON TEMPERANCE.

Whereas The rum power is being felt in the cottage of the indigent, and in the parlors of the opulent. Seemingly abrogating the labors of the philanthropist; thus sacrificing the efforts of the best minds the world has ever produced. And,

Whereas; Temperance work is becoming general all around us, yet we are not unconscious of the fact that the rum power claims to be gathering new strength and is fortifying against every means used for its suppression. And,

Whereas, The Supreme Court of Ohio has decided that we have a right to prohibit the manufacture and sale of alcoholic poison within the State. Therefore,

Resolved: That we are encouraged in the success of temperance work, because we are not required to attack this monster single handed. But with organized effort and certain work are advancing upon the foe

Resolved 2. That we recognize as auxilaries in this work, moral and legal suasion, the church, the college and the district school, and while we stand in the front of the battle these will support upon our right and left.

Resolved 3 That we will continue our united efforts with firm determination, with individual and organized effort, to storm the bulwarks, of appetite and law until this gigantic evil is removed and victory manifests itself to us in the establishment of constitutional prohibition.

Respectfully submitted,

S. A. MYERS, Committee.

CHURCH COMMISSION.

Whereas, Our general conference, at its last session appointed a church commission to prepare improvements in our constitution and confession of faith, and,

Whereas, Said action of the conference has caused some dissatisfaction; therefore

Resolved, That we, as a conference, regard said action as legitimate, and further, that said commission shall have our prayers and co-operation so for as their work may harmonize with the word of God.

On the 15th of September, 1886, the conference met in Bascom, Seneca County, to hold its fifty-fourth session, and was opened by Bishop J. Dixon by the usual services. One of the most important acts of this conference was, the adopting of lay deligation, which it did by a vote of 47 to 20. At a number of conferences the subject had been brought up but had failed to receive the necessary majority, but from this time forward the laity are to be represented in these annual gathers, and may we not hope that this action of the conference will bring about increased interest and liberality upon the part of the laity to the various interests of the church. The following brethren were licensed to preach: T. H. Ketring, J. Sheller, W. C. Needles, E. R. Horton, A. J. Burket, C. Steffy and J. E. Alspaugh; J. T. Reynolds on transfer.

Again, we were reminded of the fact that death was thining our ranks by the removing of two of our aged brethren, F. Clymer and E. M. Bell. The committee on memoirs made the following report which was adopted by the conference:

REPORT ON MEMOIRS.

We your committee on memoirs, submit the following report:

Death has again invaded our ranks, and two of our number Rev. F. Clymer and E. M. Bell have passed from labor to reward. Rev. F. Clymer was born in Franklin County, Ohio, and died at his home in Galion, Ohio, May 9th, 1886, aged 72 years, 4 months, and 24 days. He was blest with a christian home; his father Rev. John Clymer being one of the pioneer ministers of the church, where he received those religious instructions, which laid the foundation for the success that attended his labors in future life. At the age of 14 was converted to God and joined the church, which relation remained unbroken until called to join the church triumphant.

At the age of 18 he entered the work of the ministry, and until disqualified by age and infirmity continued to preach the gospel, either as an itinerant or in a local relation. He was an examplary christian and a faithful and able preacher of the word; as a revivalist few men will have more sheaves at the harvest home than he. As he approached the valley of the shadow of death he realized that the Savior which he so often recommended to others proved to be his comfort and solace in death.

Rev. E. M. Bell died at his home, near Cardington, Oct —, 1885, at the age of 72 years. Of this dear brother we can say but little, for want of proper statistics. He received his early religious training and entered the ministry in a sister church from which he came to us and was received into the Sandusky Conference, held at Gilboa, Putnam County, Oct. 1849 He entered at once the itinerancy receiving as his first appointment Salem Circuit, and become one of our most efficient and successful revivalists, receiving as high as one hundred into the church in a single year. He filled some of our most important stations, and that of Presiding Elder with great acceptibility to the people. He was a man of undoubted piety, an agreeable companion in the work of the ministry, a wise counseler, and a liberal supporter of the church. Life's battles have been fought, her victories won, and he has entered into rest. A degree of sadness comes over us as we see our ranks depleted by this common destroyer; but we hope to meet them again when life's short day shall have closed.

In view of the departure from our midst of these fathers and fellow workers, we recommend the adoption of the following resolutions:

First—That while we deeply feel their loss we meekly bow to the providence of God who doeth all things well, praying him to endow us with His holy spirit that we may imitate their example.

Second—That we tender to the aged companions of our deceased brethren our heartfelt sympathy, and pray that God may comfort and sustain them in this, the hour of their bereavement.

We recommend that some suitable remarks be made by brothers Biddle and Martin as to the life and labors of the deceased.

WM. MATHERS.
A. BIDDLE.

Remarks were made on the life and death of the deceased members of this body by A. Biddle and W. Martin. After the remarks the Conference joined in singing:

"Sweeping through the gates," etc.

The conference met to hold its fifty-fifth session in Bloomville, Seneca Co., September 29th, 1887. Bishop N. Castle being present opened the conference by singing, prayer and appropriate remarks. The following brethren were received: Henry Snyder and Joseph Losh, and H. S. Shaffer on his transfer from Michigan Conference. Thirty three lay delegates answered to their names who took a lively interest in the business, showing their appreciation of the privilege granted them by the conference.

The following report on memoirs was adopted after appropriate remarks were made by those appointed.

REPORT OF THE COMMITTEE ON MEMOIRS.

We your Committee on Memoirs would submit the following report:

Death has again invaded our ranks and three of our number, viz., John Powell, Elias Rex and Samuel Long has fallen as his victims. Rev. J. Powell died at the age of sixty-six years, on the 29th of November. He moved from Fairfield Co., to Hancock Co., in 1844. At the early age of eighteen he was converted to God and two years later was licensed to preach the gospel of Christ. For a number of year, he was a faithful and successful itinerant preacher. For the few last years of his life he was disqualified, by bodily infirmities for preaching, or to take any active part in church work, yet we cherish the hope that that gospel which he so faithfully preached to others, proved to him a solace in the hour of death. His death was somewhat sudden yet we have reason to believe that it found him ready to enter the rest prepared for the people of God.

Rev. E. Rex was born in Cumberland Co., Pennsylvania, May 11th, 1826, and died in Allen Co., April 17th., 1886, aged sixty years, eleven months and six days. He was converted when about fifteen years of age and was brought into the spiritual kingdom of Christ, and in 1851 identified himself with the church of the United Brethren in Christ. He was impressed soon after his conversion that he ought to enter the ministry, but was detered from following out his convictions by want of suitable qualification until in 1863 on the death of Rev. T. T. Rose, he was appointed by the Presiding Elder to serve out the remaining part of the year. He continued to travel up to 1876, the last two years of which were spent on Bluffton Mission, where by the blessing of God he was successful in bringing about eighty into the church. The remaining years of his life were spent in a local relation; he did not lose his interest in the cause of Christ, and from the testimony of living witnesses, we know that he passed away with the full assurance of a blessed immortality.

Rev. S. Long was born September 22d, 1801, and died at his home near Kansas, Seneca Co., September 2d, 1887, his age at the time of his death being eighty-five years, eleven months and ten days. He was converted when about eighteen years of age, and entered the itinerancy in the Muskingum Conference in 1830. He moved into the bounds of the Sandusky Conference in 1843 and the following year entered the itinerancy in this conference and was elected Presiding Elder which office he held for four years. He continued to travel up to 1856, from which time he sustained a local relation until called to his home on high. He was reserved in conversation, a man of deep piety and was recognized by all who knew him as an able preacher and most devoted servant of God, although for eight years a constant sufferer unable to converse with his friends or feed himself, during all these years of suffering he was never heard to murmur or complain but waited patiently the Lord's own time. In the removal of these dear brethren and fathers from our midst, we fully recognize the hand of our Heavenly Father and bow with humble submission to His divine will saying with his servant of old: "The Lord gave and the Lord hath taken away and blessed be the name of the Lord." We also extend to the families of our deceased brethren our heart felt sympathies, and shall pray that when life's work is over they may be united in that place prepared by the Savior for all that love him.

We recommend that some suitable remarks be made by the following brethren In the case of J. Powell, T. J. Harbaugh; in the case of E. Rex, A. W. Holden; in the case of S. Long, Wm. Mathers.

J. FRENCH.
WM. MATHERS.

The conference now numbers 90 preachers and 7762 members an increase over last year of 212. Collected for missions $2,824.85 and total for all purposes $4,5164 46.

Since the organization of the Sandusky conference we have had enrolled upon the conference journal 376 names, but where are they now? Many of them have fallen in the midst of the battle for souls, to receive the victor's crown.

"After life's fitful dream they sleep well."

Some have gone to labor in other departments of the Lord's vineyard, while a few have made shipwreck of faith to mingle again with the enemies of Christ. Death has not confined its ravages to the old, but many in the midst of their years and usefulness have fallen, such as Bright, Bowser, Rose, Coulter, Casy, Bevington, Faus and Clippinger. Their exemplary lives, and triumphant deaths, give to us new inspiration to toil on in the vineyard of the Master until called to join the immortal throng in the city of our God, to enjoy forever, that rest which remains for the people of God.

I verily believe, that when the books shall be opened the record will show, that this United Brethren Church has won as many souls to Christ according to her numbers as any other church in the land. It is a source of comfort and joy to us whose sun is rapidly sinking behind the western hills to know, that God is filling up the depleted ranks with a class of noble young men; young men that promise grand results for the church and for God. If they continue as they have begun, the future prosperity of the church will not be a matter of uncertainty, but a positive fact. In the hands of such we can die without anxiety, knowing that our church is safe.

And now, dear brethren, may we not hope that with the increased facilities for doing good, that you will carry forward the work with increasing success, commenced by the Fathers, proving yourselves worthy sons of such noble sires.

> "Oh, let us still proceed
> In Jesus' work below;
> And following our trumphant Head,
> To further conquests go."

"Now unto him that is able to keep you from falling, and to present you faultless before the presence of his glory with exceeding joy. To the only wise God our Saviour, be glory and majesty, dominion and power, both now and ever. Amen."

www.ingramcontent.com/pod-product-compliance
Lightning Source LLC
Chambersburg PA
CBHW021947160426
43195CB00011B/1260